Slater
Nursing Competencies
Rating Scale

SLATER
NURSING COMPETENCIES
RATING SCALE

MABEL A. WANDELT, R.N., Ph.D.

Professor and Assistant Dean
College of Nursing
University of Delaware
Newark, Delaware

DORIS SLATER STEWART, R.N., M.S.

Associate Professor
College of Nursing
Wayne State University
Detroit, Michigan

APPLETON-CENTURY-CROFTS/ New York
A Publishing Division of Prentice-Hall, Inc.

RT
82
W 35
X

Library of Congress Cataloging in Publication Data

Wandelt, Mabel A. 1917–
    Slater nursing competencies rating scale.

    Bibliography: p.
    1. Nurses and nursing—Ability testing. I. Stewart,
Doris Slater, joint author. II. Title. III. Title:
Nursing competencies rating scale. [DNLM: 1. Nursing
care. 2. Psychological tests. WY16 W245s]
RT82.W35   153.9'4'61073   75-4793
ISBN 0-8385-8581-7

Copyright © 1975 by APPLETON-CENTURY-CROFTS
A Publishing Division of Prentice-Hall, Inc.

75 76 77 78 79 / 10 9 8 7 6 5 4 3 2 1

PRINTED IN THE UNITED STATES OF AMERICA

ACKNOWLEDGMENTS

We owe.

We are in the debt of half the people we have known and associated with during the ten years since the Scale first appeared on paper. It is impossible to know all the persons who have contributed to the development of the Scale; the number of those who are known permits mentioning only a small portion of them. Yet, as with all projects in which the developers are debtors, it is imperative that there be some public expression of thanks to some individuals.

The first to be mentioned must be the seven faculty members of the Centralized Instructional Program for Psychiatric Nursing, Wayne State University, College of Nursing, who, with the Director, Miss Doris Haid, did the original tests of the Scale. For two years, each instructor rated each of her eight students every two weeks. It was data from their ratings that first confirmed the value and potential usefulness of the Scale.

The schools whose students participated in the Centralized Instructional Program were:

- Henry Ford Hospital School of Nursing, Detroit
- Hackley Hospital School of Nursing, Muskegan
- Harper Hospital School of Nursing, Detroit
- Mercy Central School of Nursing, Grand Rapids

The directors of the schools each secured $1,500 for a fund to support research in the program, including testing of the Scale. Perhaps more important than the funding, they encouraged faculties of their schools to test the Scale. The faculties, despite their having developed rating scales of their own, performed hundreds of ratings with the Slater Scale. These were the first tests in the clinical areas: medical-surgical, pediatrics, and maternity. Obviously, their contributions were invaluable.

Dean Emeritus Katherine E. Faville and Professor Margaret L. Shetland, former dean, of the College of Nursing not only permitted our prolonged work on the Scale, but offered encouragement to us and to the more than 50 faculty colleagues who joined in our work. These fellow faculty members devoted various amounts of time and effort to refining and testing the Scale. The confidence we had in the value of the Scale, which sustained us in our persistence with the work, was due in large part to opinions and encouragement from them. It was their work, along with that of the faculties mentioned above, that assured the content validity of the Scale and its applicability in all clinical settings.

Dr. Joel W. Ager collaborated in many aspects of testing the Scale; he was an active participant and guide in all statistical testing.

Dr. Maeona Jacobs and Miss Margory Fields did much of the handling of data for analysis and wrestled with the problems of computer programming. In addition, Miss Fields developed a plan for scaling scores, with a view for providing a valid means for ascribing college credit for knowledge and skills of clinical nursing practice. Unfortunately, the plan has not been tested.

Mrs. Gerry Jump and Mrs. Diana Perkins did the early test for internal consistency and discovered the relationship between the number of cues per item and the use of the "Not Observed" column in the Scale, which led to the expanded Cue Sheet. Their work is described in detail in their masters theses.

Mrs. Virginia Rice tested the shadowing technique for on-the-spot ratings. Concomitantly, she secured data that demonstrated the effectiveness of the Scale for measurements of competencies displayed by staff nurses and data demonstrating that the Scale discriminates among students at various levels in the curriculum.

Section VIII, page 89, reports results of use of the Scale by others and purposes of various types of studies in which it has been used. The nursing staff of the Veterans Administration Hospital, Little Rock, Arkansas, were first to use it in a service setting; they employed the Scale to measure the effects of reorganization of the nursing service program. The studies reported are only a few that have been shared with us. A thousand or more schools of nursing and nursing care agencies have examined the Scale, and many use it in continuing evaluation programs.

We have noted names of a few persons and a few groups. To these we extend once more an expression of thanks for their faith, interest, assistance, and encouragement. They must serve as the representatives of all ratees, raters, and supporters of our work.

I have spoken for Doris Slater Stewart and myself in our acknowledgement of debt and expression of gratitude to all who have shared the adventure of developing the Scale. I speak for myself and for all users of the Scale, including ratees who can know more about themselves as nurses, when I express debt and gratitude to Doris Slater Stewart for her construction of the Scale and her original thinking, which is the essence of the value of the Scale. I must tell of

Doris's sharing her work with me, her nonpossessiveness in permitting varied small modifications I wanted, and her tireless work in promotion of the many testing chores. I am in debt, we are in debt, to Doris Slater Stewart.

The work of the development and testing of the Scale was supported, in part, by funds from Faculty Research Development Grant NU00163, from the Division of Nursing, Department of Health, Education, and Welfare.

M.A.W.

PREFACE

The multipage rating scale is placed immediately following brief introductory materials because it, in itself, can best serve to identify what the Slater Nursing Competencies Scale is.

The 22-page Cue Sheet follows immediately (p. 9) because it has been demonstrated to be an essential feature in assuring full utilization of the scale.

Section III, Instructions for Use of the Scale (p. 33), provides what-to-do instructions, along with the rationales underlying some of them. In most instances the Scale will be used to do ratings in retrospect; for some purposes, it may be desirable to conduct on-the-spot ratings, using a shadowing technique. Each method is described.

Section IV, Standard of Measurement and the Ratings (p. 43), presents ideas germane to making judgments and ascribing ratings. These ideas enhance the self-confidence of raters using the Slater Scale and offer understanding of subjectivity and objectivity in judgment. Also discussed is the need to hold a standard of measurement constant, which is in contrast to use of the flexible or sliding standard of measurement that is characteristic of most tools developed to measure clinical nursing performance.

Section V, Tests of the Scale (p. 53), describes briefly the results of various statistical testings.

Section VI, Measurement for Evaluation (p. 59), is an essay describing a systematic approach to planning for evaluation. It serves as a guide to procedure regardless of the purposes for which information is being sought: whether it be to compare persons or situations that vary in time or setting, or to determine the extent to which program objectives have been achieved. Though much of this section is explanation and direction, it is called an essay because it urges evaluators to pursue a systematic approach when engaging in any evaluation endeavor. In some aspects, the process may seem unnecessarily detailed. The argument is that the seemingly lengthy route is the shortest course to assurance that the measurements (information) obtained are relevant to the purpose for which the information is sought.

Section VII, The Essay as Background (p. 81), identifies and describes some ways in which background ideas from the essay can serve as guides and rationale for particular applications of the Slater Scale.

Section VIII, Others' Experiences with the Slater Scale (p. 89), reports a few examples of use of the Slater Scale for instructional and research purposes.

The Appendix provides a fold-out copy of the scale in a size convenient for use. Users may reproduce any number of copies, as needed for their evaluation projects.

Because of extensive interest in the Scale as an instrument yielding highly useful measurements of clinical nursing performance, the Scale, Cue Sheet, and an early draft of guidelines for use have been supplied at cost by the College of Nursing, Wayne State University, to persons who inquired about it. Many schools of nursing and nursing service agencies have used the Scale in their evaluation programs. The feedback from the experiences of many of the users has aided in the improvement of the instructions for use, and prompted the addition of Sections V, VI, and VII. The early draft of instructions was ample to permit use of the Scale, though many were concerned about the limited information about testing and many could not see how the measurements would serve to evaluate attainment of their program objectives.

The current publication differs markedly from the early draft in the following ways:

1. The instructions for use have been completely revised.
2. Tests of the Scale, a section of particular importance to program directors and researchers, is included.
3. There are entirely new sections on subjectivity and objectivity in judgment, ideas about holding constant the standard of measurement, and measurement for evaluation, which includes guides to defining goal-identifying terms to assure selection of relevant criterion measures.
4. The reports of use by others offer evidence of usefulness and suggestions of applicability of the Scale to varied situations and needs.
5. Permission is granted to users to reproduce copies of the scale as needed for any particular evaluation project.

CONTENTS

INTRODUCTION

The Slater Nursing Competencies Rating Scale can be introduced briefly under the headings: What It Is, What It Does, and What Purposes It Serves.

WHAT IT IS

The Slater Scale is a scale consisting of 84 items which identify actions performed by nursing personnel as they provide care for patients. The standard of measurement is the "quality of performance of care expected of a first-level staff nurse"; the standard of measurement is held constant for all measurements made with the Scale. The concept of and rationale behind the standard of measurement are discussed in detail in Section IV (p. 43). The total composition of the Scale includes the 6-page listing of the 84 items, along with space for recording ratings; the 22-page Cue Sheet, which lists several concrete examples of activities illustrative of each item; and the Instructions for Use of the Scale. The items are arranged into six subsections, according to the primary-science and cultural bases for the nursing care actions to be rated:

Subsection		Number of Items
I	*Psychosocial: Individual* – Actions directed toward meeting psychosocial needs of individual patients	18
II	*Psychosocial: Group* – Actions directed toward meeting psychosocial needs of patients as members of a group	13
III	*Physical* – Actions directed toward meeting physical needs of patients	13
IV	*General* – Actions that may be directed toward meeting either psychosocial or physical needs of patients, or both at the same time	16

WHAT IT DOES

The Slater Scale measures the competencies displayed by a nurse as she performs nursing actions in providing care to patients. The Scale may be used in any setting where nurses intervene in behalf of patients, either in direct nurse-patient interactions or in other interventions. The Scale yields both numerical and descriptive information. The numerical scores provide data that permit statistical analyses to be used in comparison and hypothesis-testing studies. The descriptive findings provide information that can be used either directly or by interpretation as a basis for planning means to improvement. In other words, the information gained from measurements made with the Slater Scale not only provides means for accounting for the quality of a nursing staff's performance and for identifying areas of strengths and weaknesses, but also provides descriptions of the strengths and weaknesses which serve directly for planning ways to strengthen and improve the quality of nurse performance. The Scale repeatedly has been demonstrated to be sensitive enough to measure changes that occur (learning) in as brief a time as two weeks.

WHAT PURPOSES IT SERVES

Among the purposes for which measurements from the Slater Scale may serve are:

1. Periodically to evaluate individual nurses, where retention, promotion, and merit salary increases are among the considerations;
2. To allow administration to examine the relationship between the quality of performance by nurses and the quality of care received by patients;
3. To identify areas of needed instruction for in-service educational programs or particular learning needs of individuals or selected groups of staff members;
4. To follow student progress in a particular course of study (repeated use), or to evaluate student achievement after completion of a course or total program;
5. To measure nurse competence as a basis for ascribing college credit by examination;
6. To guide in self-evaluation;
7. To determine through research the effects of different instructional approaches.

The items are constructed so as to describe observable nurse actions, which enables users to match them readily with criterion measures for the behaviorally stated objectives of any program designed to modify nursing performance.

The Slater Scale — unlike most measurement devices, which indicate only a particular level of attainment — provides a means to follow progressive achievement. Course grades merely tell a student that she has or has not maintained a particular level of achievement. The Slater Scale will tell her the degree to which she increases her competency as a nurse at successive points during her years in an educational program. This feature can serve nursing service administration by providing information about increases in staff competence to be used for planning salary schedules.

FEATURES MAKING FOR EFFECTIVENESS

Two features of the standard of measurement make for its universal applicability: (1) the familiarity of users with the idea of the performance expected of a first-level staff nurse and (2) the holding constant of the standard of measurement. When new measuring devices are developed, it is best to employ for the standard of measurement an object or phenomenon that is readily understood and available to most potential users. The standards for many commonly used measuring devices were based on readily available objects: the yard and foot as measures of linear distance; the stone as a measure of weight; horsepower as a measure of energy; the calorie as a measure of heat; and many others. For the Slater Scale, the standard of measurement selected is "the performance expected of a first-level staff nurse," a phenomenon familiar and readily available to nurses concerned with measurement of the competence of a person who provides nursing care for patients.

The second feature, holding constant the standard of measurement, even more than the common understanding of the standard of measurement itself, is the feature that renders the scale universally applicable. It is this feature that provides measurements that can be compared to determine whether differences or similarities of competence exist among various persons providing care in varied situations. These two features are discussed in greater detail in the section Standard of Measurement and the Ratings (pp. 43-52).

SECTION I

The Slater
Nursing Competencies
Rating Scale

Date:

SLATER NURSING COMPETENCIES RATING SCALE

Nurse being rated: Rater (name or No.):

PSYCHOSOCIAL: INDIVIDUAL

Actions directed toward meeting psychosocial
needs of individual patients.

Column headers (diagonal): BEST NURSE / BETWEEN / AVERAGE NURSE / BETWEEN / POOREST NURSE / NOT APPLICABLE / NOT OBSERVED

1. Gives full attention to patient   ( ) ___ ( ) ___ ( ) ___ ___

2. Is a receptive listener   ( ) ___ ( ) ___ ( ) ___ ___

3. Approaches patient in a kind, gentle,
    and friendly manner   ( ) ___ ( ) ___ ( ) ___ ___

4. Responds in a therapeutic manner to
    patient's behavior   ( ) ___ ( ) ___ ( ) ___ ___

5. Recognizes anxiety in patient and
    takes appropriate action   ( ) ___ ( ) ___ ( ) ___ ___

6. Gives explanation and verbal reassurance
    when needed   ( ) ___ ( ) ___ ( ) ___ ___

7. Offers companionship to patient without
    becoming involved in a nontherapeutic
    way   ( ) ___ ( ) ___ ( ) ___ ___

8. Considers patient as a member of a
    family and of society   ( ) ___ ( ) ___ ( ) ___ ___

9. Is alert to patient's spiritual needs   ( ) ___ ( ) ___ ( ) ___ ___

10. Identifies individual needs expressed
    through behavior and initiates actions
    to meet them   ( ) ___ ( ) ___ ( ) ___ ___

11. Accepts rejection or ridicule and
    continues effort to meet needs   ( ) ___ ( ) ___ ( ) ___ ___

12. Communicates belief in the worth and
    dignity of man   ( ) ___ ( ) ___ ( ) ___ ___

13. Utilizes healthy aspects of patient's
    personality   ( ) ___ ( ) ___ ( ) ___ ___

14. Creates an atmosphere of mutual trust,
    acceptance, and respect, rather than
    showing concern for power, prestige,
    and authority   ( ) ___ ( ) ___ ( ) ___ ___

NOTE: To facilitate identification, Best, Average, and Poorest Nurse columns are marked with parentheses.

	BEST NURSE	BETWEEN	AVERAGE NURSE	BETWEEN	POOREST NURSE	NOT APPLICABLE	NOT OBSERVED

15. Is well informed about current events and common interests that can be shared with patient ( ) __ ( ) __ ( ) __ __

16. Chooses appropriate topics for conversation ( ) __ ( ) __ ( ) __ __

17. Offers purposeful experiences and activities that will help the patient to participate and communicate with others ( ) __ ( ) __ ( ) __ __

18. Conducts self with same professional demeanor when caring for an unconscious or nonoriented patient as when caring for a conscious patient ( ) __ ( ) __ ( ) __ __

PSYCHOSOCIAL: GROUP

Actions directed toward meeting psychosocial needs of patients as members of a group

19. Conveys warmth and interest in group situations with patients ( ) __ ( ) __ ( ) __ __

20. Helps groups of patients accept necessary limits to freedom ( ) __ ( ) __ ( ) __ __

21. Encourages patients to participate in planning their own group living experiences ( ) __ ( ) __ ( ) __ __

22. Delegates responsibility to patients according to their capabilities ( ) __ ( ) __ ( ) __ __

23. Proposes activities appropriate to interests and needs of various patients within group ( ) __ ( ) __ ( ) __ __

24. Changes activities to meet priority needs in group, even though it would be easier to continue with activity already begun ( ) __ ( ) __ ( ) __ __

25. Structures activities for the purpose of helping patients vent their emotions in a socially acceptable way ( ) __ ( ) __ ( ) __ __

26. Participates in group activities without dominating the situation ( ) __ ( ) __ ( ) __ __

27. Gives praise and recognition for achievement according to individual's needs and with respect for others in the group ( ) __ ( ) __ ( ) __ __

	BEST NURSE	BETWEEN	AVERAGE NURSE	BETWEEN	POOREST NURSE	NOT APPLICABLE	NOT OBSERVED

28. Conducts activities with enthusiasm and without emphasizing individual competition ( ) ___ ( ) ___ ( ) ___ ___

29. Converses with patients during group activities ( ) ___ ( ) ___ ( ) ___ ___

30. Shares time with all patients in group ( ) ___ ( ) ___ ( ) ___ ___

31. Guides group discussion when this is desirable ( ) ___ ( ) ___ ( ) ___ ___

PHYSICAL

Actions directed toward meeting physical needs of patients

32. Adapts nursing procedures to meet needs of individual patients for daily hygiene and for treatment ( ) ___ ( ) ___ ( ) ___ ___

33. Attends to daily hygienic needs for cleanliness and acceptable appearance ( ) ___ ( ) ___ ( ) ___ ___

34. Utilizes nursing procedures as media for communication and interaction with patients ( ) ___ ( ) ___ ( ) ___ ___

35. Identifies physical symptoms and physical changes ( ) ___ ( ) ___ ( ) ___ ___

36. Recognizes physical distress and acts to provide relief for the patient ( ) ___ ( ) ___ ( ) ___ ___

37. Encourages patient to observe adequate rest and exercise ( ) ___ ( ) ___ ( ) ___ ___

38. Encourages patient to take adequate diet ( ) ___ ( ) ___ ( ) ___ ___

39. Recognizes and reports behavioral and physiologic changes that are due to drugs ( ) ___ ( ) ___ ( ) ___ ___

40. Adjusts expectations of patient's behavior according to the effect the drug has on the patient ( ) ___ ( ) ___ ( ) ___ ___

41. Demonstrates understanding of both medical and surgical sepsis ( ) ___ ( ) ___ ( ) ___ ___

42. Recognizes hazards to patient safety and takes appropriate action to maintain a safe environment and to give patient feeling of being safe ( ) ___ ( ) ___ ( ) ___ ___

43. Carries out safety measures developed to prevent patients from harming themselves or others ( ) ___ ( ) ___ ( ) ___ ___

44. Carries out established technique for
safe administration of medications and
parenteral fluids   ( ) __ ( ) __ ( ) __ __

GENERAL

Actions that may be directed toward meeting
either psychosocial or physical needs of
patients, or both at the same time.

45. Utilizes patient teaching opportunities   ( ) __ ( ) __ ( ) __ __

46. Involves patient and family in planning
for care and treatments   ( ) __ ( ) __ ( ) __ __

47. Protects sensitivities of patient   ( ) __ ( ) __ ( ) __ __

48. Encourages patient to accept dependence/
independence as appropriate to his
condition   ( ) __ ( ) __ ( ) __ __

49. Utilizes resources within the milieu to
provide patient with opportunities for
problem solving   ( ) __ ( ) __ ( ) __ __

50. Allows patient freedom of choice in
details of daily living whenever possible
and within patient's ability to make
choice   ( ) __ ( ) __ ( ) __ __

51. Encourages patient to take part in
activities of daily living that will
stimulate his potential for positive
growth   ( ) __ ( ) __ ( ) __ __

52. Adapts activities to physical and mental
abilities of patient   ( ) __ ( ) __ ( ) __ __

53. Adapts nursing care to patient's level
and pace of development   ( ) __ ( ) __ ( ) __ __

54. Provides for diversional and treatment   ( ) __ ( ) __ ( ) __ __
activities appropriate to patient's
capabilities and needs

55. Allows for slow or unskilled performance
without showing annoyance or impatience   ( ) __ ( ) __ ( ) __ __

56. Establishes nursing care goals within
the framework of the therapist's plan
of care   ( ) __ ( ) __ ( ) __ __

57. Adapts to and works with varied
approaches to treatment   ( ) __ ( ) __ ( ) __ __

58. Relates to patient within the framework
of the therapeutic plan   ( ) ___ ( ) ___ ( ) ___ ___

59. Carries out watchfulness in an
unobtrusive manner   ( ) ___ ( ) ___ ( ) ___ ___

60. Responds appropriately to emergency
situations   ( ) ___ ( ) ___ ( ) ___ ___

COMMUNICATION

Communication on behalf of patients

61. Communicates ideas, facts, feelings,
and concepts clearly in speech   ( ) ___ ( ) ___ ( ) ___ ___

62. Communicates ideas, facts, feelings, and
concepts clearly in writing   ( ) ___ ( ) ___ ( ) ___ ___

63. Establishes a well-developed nursing
care plan   ( ) ___ ( ) ___ ( ) ___ ___

64. Gives accurate reports, verbal and
written, of patient's behavior, including
behavior that involved interaction with
self   ( ) ___ ( ) ___ ( ) ___ ___

65. Participates freely in ward patient-
care conferences   ( ) ___ ( ) ___ ( ) ___ ___

66. Communicates effectively and establishes
good relationships with other
disciplines   ( ) ___ ( ) ___ ( ) ___ ___

67. Attends to patient's needs through use
of referrals, both to departments in
the hospital as agency and to other
community agencies   ( ) ___ ( ) ___ ( ) ___ ___

PROFESSIONAL IMPLICATIONS

Actions directed toward fulfilling responsibilities
of a nurse in all facets and varieties of patient-
care situations.

68. Is self-directing: takes initiative and
goes ahead on own   ( ) ___ ( ) ___ ( ) ___ ___

69. Makes decisions willingly and
appropriately   ( ) ___ ( ) ___ ( ) ___ ___

70. Makes decisions that reflect both
knowledge of facts and good judgment   ( ) ___ ( ) ___ ( ) ___ ___

	BEST NURSE	BETWEEN	AVERAGE NURSE	BETWEEN	POOREST NURSE	NOT APPLICABLE	NOT OBSERVED

71. Gives verbal evidence of good insight into deeper problems and needs of patients   ( ) ___ ( ) ___ ( ) ___ ___

72. Contributes as nurse member of health team to planning and evaluating care   ( ) ___ ( ) ___ ( ) ___ ___

73. Spends time with patients, rather than with other nurses or hospital personnel   ( ) ___ ( ) ___ ( ) ___ ___

74. Reliable: follows through with responsibilities   ( ) ___ ( ) ___ ( ) ___ ___

75. Stays with assigned patients, or knows where and how they are   ( ) ___ ( ) ___ ( ) ___ ___

76. Impresses others with sincerity of interest and nursing effort   ( ) ___ ( ) ___ ( ) ___ ___

77. Gives continued interest and encouragement to various-level programs, whether directed to care of patients of her immediate concern or institution-wide programs   ( ) ___ ( ) ___ ( ) ___ ___

78. Participates in staff meetings   ( ) ___ ( ) ___ ( ) ___ ___

79. Avails self of opportunities for learning   ( ) ___ ( ) ___ ( ) ___ ___

80. Is a good follower (helpful, cooperative)   ( ) ___ ( ) ___ ( ) ___ ___

81. Is a good leader (constructive)   ( ) ___ ( ) ___ ( ) ___ ___

82. Is helpful to ward personnel   ( ) ___ ( ) ___ ( ) ___ ___

83. Cooperates with ward routines and hospital regulations   ( ) ___ ( ) ___ ( ) ___ ___

84. Accepts authority situations with understanding   ( ) ___ ( ) ___ ( ) ___ ___

SECTION II

Cue Sheet

PSYCHOSOCIAL: INDIVIDUAL

Actions directed toward meeting psychosocial needs of individual patients.

1. **Gives Full Attention to Patient.**
   a. Is alert and responds verbally and nonverbally without asking patient to repeat phrases.
   b. Assumes positions that will aid in observation and communication with patient.
   c. Restricts talking to conversation with patient as she carries out activities for his care; avoids chitchat with other personnel.
   d. Looks at and talks to infant as she gives bottle feeding.
   e. Poses questions encouraging patient to express feelings.

2. **Is a Receptive Listener.**
   a. Facial expression indicates interest and understanding.
   b. Gives patient time to talk.
   c. Waits for patient to complete sentence before speaking or moving away from patient.
   d. Encourages conversation by using brief comments or leading questions to let patient know she is listening and interested.
   e. Terminates conversation in manner such that patient understands reason for termination, leaving patient with feeling of satisfaction about discussion.

3. **Approaches Patient in a Kind, Gentle, and Friendly Manner.**
   a. Speaks clearly, with soft and pleasant tone of voice.
   b. Calls patient by name and tells her name, enunciating distinctly.
   c. Shows patience and understanding with repeated complaints or with crying of patients (all ages).
   d. Invites approach of patients with a smile and encouraging word.

4. **Responds in a Therapeutic Manner to Patient's Behavior.**
   a. Assists withdrawn patient to consider various means for involvement or interactions with others.
   b. Redirects attention of adolescent who is teasing others and interfering with activities of others.
   c. Helps patient who refuses examination or treatment to think through various facets and alternatives in the situation.
   d. Accepts expressions of hostility and makes changes that can be made, explains why some things cannot be changed, and indicates to the patient that she is interested in knowing his feelings.

5. **Recognizes Anxiety in Patient and Takes Appropriate Action.**
    a. Asks leading questions to determine what patient knows about pending surgery and to allow him to express fears.
    b. Encourages laboring mother to express her thoughts and feelings about impending delivery, her own safety, and the health of her baby.
    c. Spends time with patient or arranges to have someone stay with anxious patient.
    d. Attempts to learn from parents things that child fears and actions that help to alleviate his fears.
    e. Allows and assists patient to talk of disfigurement or death, to express thoughts and feelings about them.

6. **Gives Explanation and Verbal Reassurance When Needed.**
    a. Uses leading questions to determine what patient knows about illness and treatment, and offers elaboration as needed.
    b. Attempts to describe kind of pain or discomfort patient may anticipate; includes estimate of duration of discomfort and what will be done and what patient might do to alleviate pain or distress.
    c. Helps patient explore and understand why he feels about or behaves as he does toward other persons, toward himself, or toward his illness.
    d. Comments about patient's actions to remind and reassure him of signs of movement toward wellness.

7. **Offers Companionship to Patient Without Becoming Involved in a Non-therapeutic Way.**
    a. Maintains nurse-patient relationship (avoiding friend-friend relationship) by focusing on patient's interests.
    b. Provides for child's needs for affection and closeness, but helps child to remember parents and siblings.
    c. Maintains use of appropriate names of address, both those she uses for patient and those patient uses to address her.
    d. Avoids monopoly of time – the patient, hers; or she, the patient's.
    e. Encourages and listens to patient considering alternate actions, but allows patient to make own decision.

8. **Considers Patient as a Member of a Family and of Society.**
    a. Provides care and treatment activities at times that will least interfere with visiting family or friends.
    b. Encourages family to participate in care of patient.
    c. Assists patient to maintain communication with friends and colleagues – comfortable setting for visitors, assistance with telephoning, positioning and materials for letter writing, prompt mail delivery.

d. Discusses current news, with particular focus on items known to be of interest to patient.

e. Discusses ways of coping with aftercare.

9. **Is Alert to Patient's Spiritual Needs.**

   a. Respects patient's religious beliefs; listens respectfully if patient wishes to talk about religious beliefs or feelings.

   b. Handles religious articles with respect.

   c. Communicates promptly with pastor when patient expresses desire to see him, or volunteers to call pastor.

   d. Offers assistance and encourages patient to attend services of his faith that are available to him (within the limits of his physical ability to do so).

10. **Identifies Individual Needs Expressed Through Behavior and Initiates Actions to Meet Them.**

    a. Notes when patient makes repeated reference to a topic and encourages him to discuss it.

    b. Spends time with patient who has no visitors and is interfering with visiting of other patients.

    c. Arranges with local volunteers to visit older patient who detains her, obviously just to visit.

    d. Encourages patient who disagrees or finds fault with plans and actions of others to suggest some procedures for activities in which he must be involved.

11. **Accepts Rejection or Ridicule and Continues Effort to Meet Needs.**

    a. Returns frequently to patient who refuses to talk; displays interested manner and gives assurance of "being there."

    b. Displays willingness to understand patient's point of view in relation to refused activity or treatment.

    c. Stays with patient who turns away or shouts, "Go away," speaking quietly and reassuringly, helping with resolution of need to reject attention offered.

    d. Attempts to help patient clarify his understanding of rationale for nurse actions or for treatments she proposes.

12. **Communicates Belief in the Worth and Dignity of Man.**

    a. Cares for all patients with kindness and helpfulness.

    b. Encourages withdrawn patient to make choices about daily care and allows time for patient to make decision and respond.

    c. Endeavors to meet all requests and needs of hopelessly ill or dying patient with same display of interest in the individual as that shown other patients.

    d. Addresses each patient by name and refers to patient by name when discussing him with colleagues.

13. **Utilizes Healthy Aspects of Patient's Personality.**
    a. Uses patient's resources in problem resolution; e.g., guiding patient to consider various alternatives in arriving at a decision, before patient can experience frustration at his inability to decide.
    b. Provides opportunities for patient to receive satisfaction through contribution to others; e.g., having child in wheelchair take toy to child confined to bed.
    c. Is quick to point out patient's abilities, while avoiding focus on his disabilities.
    d. Encourages and provides ways for patient to enlarge his knowledge in areas that are of interest to him.

14. **Creates an Atmosphere of Mutual Trust, Acceptance, and Respect, Rather Than Showing Concern for Power, Prestige, and Authority.**
    a. Trusts the patient in as many ways as possible — does not let own anxieties limit patient activities.
    b. Accepts patient as an individual, allows him to express opinions without argument or defensiveness.
    c. Minimizes conversations dwelling on status of nurse or other personnel.
    d. Indicates respect for patient by way she addresses him, by tone of voice; avoids being disruptive to patient's conversation or activities and expects in return the usual amount of respect from the patient.
    e. Quietly and briefly points out inappropriate comments or actions made by the patient.

15. **Is Well Informed About Current Events and Common Interests That Can Be Shared with Patient.**
    a. Knows results of latest sports event; who won the "Oscars" the previous evening; outcomes of yesterday's elections; current status of strike negotiations; names of latest best-selling book, record, movie.
    b. Encourages patient to describe or discuss recent events; may use this route to furthering her own knowledge, though the purpose for so doing would be to involve patient in healthy pursuit.
    c. Brings bit of information to patient in relation to known interest of the patient.

16. **Chooses Appropriate Topics for Conversation.**
    a. Introduces topics of known interest to patient: particular sport, hobby, TV show, doll, or neighborhood activity.
    b. Encourages patient to talk about personal interests and concerns; e.g., children, family, and what family is probably doing at home.
    c. Guides conversation to neutral or positive subject, should an argument develop or seem to be developing.

17. **Offers Purposeful Experiences and Activities That Will Help the Patient to Participate and Communicate with Others.**
    a. Makes arrangements for patients to have meals at tables shared by three or four others.
    b. Has patients who have "been through it" talk with patient anticipating treatment or rehabilitation activity.
    c. Suggests that accomplished knitter assist patient learning to knit.
    d. Makes certain that patient knows names of patients in beds on either side of him.

18. **Conducts Self with Same Professional Demeanor When Caring for an Unconscious or Nonoriented Patient as When Caring for a Conscious Patient.**
    a. Seeks assistance in moving the patient and performs moving in safe, gentle manner.
    b. Maintains focus of conversation with co-workers on matters about the patient and his immediate care; avoids jocularity.
    c. In patient's presence, refers to patient by name, speaks in well-modulated tone, avoids discussion of patient's condition or prognosis.
    d. Informs nonoriented patient about anticipated treatments, offers instructions about what will be expected of patient, conveys attitude of interest in helping patient to understand.

PSYCHOSOCIAL: GROUP

Actions directed toward meeting psychosocial needs of patients as members of a group.

19. **Conveys Warmth and Interest in Group Situations with Patients.**
    a. Listens to conversation when she first approaches group, enters discussion with comments that promote continuation of patients' interests.
    b. Inquires about interests of group, listens to responses.

   c. Proposes ways to promote activities suggested by members of group, rather than proposing alternative activities.
   d. Sits down as a member of group.
   e. Communicates with all members of group, avoiding addressing self to a particular member.

20. **Helps Groups of Patients Accept Necessary Limits to Freedom.**
   a. Early in discussion of plans for group activities, identifies limits and allows discussion of reasons for the limitations.
   b. Identifies reasons for limitations that relate to needs of patients as well as those related to "regulations."
   c. Helps group of adolescents plan games that permit participation of few with physical limitations, without placing undue attention on individuals with the limitations.
   d. Accepts hostile expressions related to limits, but remains firm and consistent in maintaining necessary limits.

21. **Encourages Patients to Participate in Planning Their Own Group Living Experiences.**
   a. Helps patients plan task assignments and rotation of assignments.
   b. Encourages patients to suggest routines, activities, time schedules, etc.
   c. Seeks patients' suggestions and assistance in making changes in physical setting — furniture arrangement, room assignments, etc.
   d. Brings patients into early planning stages for all "social" activities, such as supper on the lawn, TV schedule for the week, games for late afternoon, birthday party, etc.

22. **Delegates Responsibility to Patients According to Their Capabilities.**
   a. Encourages patient to be "chairman" of committee to plan Fourth of July celebration.
   b. Suggests that aggressive patient serve as member of committee, providing support to "chairman," but not "taking over" chairman's duties.
   c. Provides patient with schedule for his examinations or treatments and suggests that he assume responsibility for being at the right place at the right time.
   d. Allows patients to initiate preparations for meals, visits, or bedtime, without reminding them each time that it is time to do these things.
   e. Gives recognition to patients by identifying strengths and offers opportunities that encourage the utilization of abilities.

23. **Proposes Activities Appropriate to Interests and Needs of Various Patients Within Group.**
   a. Notes involvement of each patient in group activity and subtly suggests

modifications to ensure appropriate involvement of all, such as proposing that the child with the injured knee keep score for the volleyball game.

b. Suggests ways of dividing group into small common-interest subgroups: playing checkers, playing pinochle, working jigsaw puzzles, playing with dolls, building with blocks, etc.

c. Suggests ways that subgroups can share interest with other groups, such as patients interested in color and design developing patterns for those interested in "production"—woodwork, needlework, clay modeling, etc.

d. Assigns activities that encourage constructive outlet for feelings; i.e., patients with aggressive tendencies who need recognition are offered opportunities to plan activities that will interest other patients.

24. **Changes Activities to Meet Priority Needs in Group, Even Though It Would Be Easier to Continue with Activity Already Begun.**

a. When two patients obviously are "ganging up" to win every game of rummy, suggests change to card game in which they are less expert or proposes change to building model cars.

b. When withdrawn patient is making no contribution to game of Scrabble, proposes change to simple card game.

c. When uncommunicative patients are "watching" television, suggests they plan furniture arrangements in anticipation of afternoon visitors.

d. Instead of continuing with a game such as volleyball that can last for an indefinite period of time whether patients are interested or not, intervenes with activities that are more individualized and demanding of nurse's time and effort.

25. **Structures Activities for the Purpose of Helping Patients Vent Their Emotions in a Socially Acceptable Way.**

a. Helps group establish guidelines and encourages discussions of emotion-laden issues; e.g., suggests that children discuss experiences, and feelings about them, with school and teachers; or suggests patients "debate" merits of various sides of political issues.

b. Develops word game where patients, each in turn, have opportunity to express first thing that comes to mind in relation to lead words.

c. Recognizes hostility and offers activities that demand physical strength, energy, and movement; i.e., a round or two with punching bag, volleyball or dodgeball.

26. **Participates in Group Activities Without Dominating the Situation.**

a. Awaits her turn along with others.

b. Allows other patients in the group to control fellow patients in process of activity, without being first to interfere with "erroneous" or disruptive action of a single participant.

    c. Allows activity to proceed along lines acceptable to patients, rather than proposing "way I would do it."

    d. Encourages hesitant patients to join activity; assists less apt patients, without actually performing for them.

27. **Gives Praise and Recognition for Achievement According to Individual's Needs and with Respect for Others in the Group.**

    a. Displays pleasure and encourages others to join rejoicing at the accomplishment of reticent patient.

    b. Moves quickly to next activity when "braggart" has scored point — helps patient recognize his accomplishment in relation to his abilities and those of others; guides him in recognizing achievements of others.

    c. Discusses and helps patient recognize relationship of small accomplishment to potential for "next (more difficult) step."

28. **Conducts Activities with Enthusiasm and Without Emphasizing Individual Competition.**

    a. Expresses enthusiasm in relation to interests of all patients in group; avoids highlighting interest of one or two patients.

    b. Involves skilled patients in assisting the less skilled, rather than allowing them to continuously demonstrate their own skill.

    c. Enlists more vocal patients as leaders of group discussions, helping them to assume appropriate role of discussion leader; i.e., drawing out expressions of opinion and information from each member of the group.

29. **Converses with Patients During Group Activities.**

    a. Encourages light conversation during meals; e.g., origins of foods or recipies, varieties of preparations of foods, what dolls like best to eat, who feeds pets, favorite foods, etc.

    b. Introduces discussion of "most interesting" item of category of items being produced: model ship, needlework, jigsaw puzzle, paper doll, room arrangement, party decorations.

    c. Points out observations that might encourage patient participation; i.e., "Your suggestions are particularly helpful to the group," or "Nice going, that was a good serve."

30. **Shares Time with All Patients in Group.**

    a. Notes withdrawn or quiet patient and physically approaches him with attention focused on what he is doing, or addresses comment or question to him.

    b. Makes point of addressing comment or question to apparently most independent patient in group, letting him know she is aware of him as an individual and of his participation and interests.

c. Gives attention to all interests expressed and asks if anyone has interests they wish to share with the group.

31. **Guides Group Discussion When This Is Desirable.**
    a. When new activity is to be introduced, informs group about it and guides discussion of feelings about activity and planning for it; e.g., breakfast is to be served one-half hour later, there will be a movie one evening a week, there will be daily visiting permitted.
    b. Guides discussion of initial planning and task assignment when group plans special holiday programs, assists with identification of necessary committees and decisions about membership of committees.

PHYSICAL

Actions directed toward meeting physical needs of patients.

32. **Adapts Nursing Procedures to Meet Needs of Individual Patients for Daily Hygiene and for Treatment.**
    a. Gives only partial soap and water bath to elderly patient with dry skin.
    b. Offers assistance with oral hygiene; e.g., prepares brush and holds basin for patient with upper extremity cast, brushes dentures under running water for patient unable to do this himself, teaches child proper brushing.
    c. Arranges equipment and materials on side of bed and in convenient position for left-handed patient to do his own tracheal suction.
    d. Leaves general morning care of arthritic patient to last, so neither will feel pressure of time and movements can be made slowly.
    e. Reduces equipment to a minimum when giving treatment to fearful, excited patients.

33. **Attends to Daily Hygienic Needs for Cleanliness and Acceptable Appearance.**
    a. Offers to comb hair of patient unable to do so for physical or mental reasons; e.g., cardiac patient, patient with upper extremity injury, patient in state of emotional shock following loss of loved ones, regressed mental patient.
    b. Helps disturbed patient select items of attire that "go together."
    c. Assist patient with plan and materials for shaving.
    d. Offers clean clothing as indicated.
    e. Provides for body, dressing, and air deodorizers, as indicated.

34. **Utilizes Nursing Procedures as Media for Communication and Interaction with Patients.**
    a. Encourages withdrawn patient to talk of self, interests, and family, while providing direct nursing care.

     b. Encourages patient to make own decisions about "what to wear today"; allows child to make own selection of clothes.

     c. Asks patient to suggest time convenient for him for particular care or treatment.

     d. Helps mother to listen to heartbeat of her unborn child and encourages her to talk about the baby and its meaning to her.

     e. Encourages patient to assist, even in a small way, with particularly painful treatment; e.g., burn dressing, repeated intramuscular injection, etc.

35. **Identifies Physical Symptoms and Physical Changes.**

     a. Notices cyanosis – checks for bleeding, oxygen flow, position in relation to breathing.

     b. Notes mottled tissues over bony prominence; increases frequency of turning patient and provides ways to keep pressure from area.

     c. Notes languor and shallow breathing of small child, takes appropriate action.

     d. Notes undesirable weight loss in elderly clinic patient; questions patient about changes in eating habits, living conditions, appetite.

36. **Recognizes Physical Distress and Acts to Provide Relief for the Patient.**

     a. Moves patient up in bed and adjusts pillows to provide support in good body alignment.

     b. Notes cramping position of extremities, changes position and provides supports for maintenance of good body alignment.

     c. Notes signs of pain – restlessness, perspiration, facial contortion – and takes action to alleviate pain; e.g., change of position, medication, fresh dressing.

37. **Encourages Patient to Observe Adequate Rest and Exercise.**

     a. Helps patient understand role of rest in his treatment – cardiac, thrombophlebitis, hepatitis.

     b. Helps patient understand role of exercise in treatment of his illness – postsurgical, paralysis, traction or cast immobilization.

     c. Assists elderly patient out of bed; encourages patient to stand and to help self. Gives patient time to do for himself, while she stands by to offer necessary assistance and protection.

     d. Helps patient plan ways to save movement and steps in accomplishing tasks of daily care.

     e. Suggests new interests to patient: reading or light handcrafts for rest; birdwatching or loom weaving for exercise.

38. **Encourages Patient to Take Adequate Diet.**

     a. Discusses eating habits with patient to learn habits and food likes and dislikes.

b. Helps patient know what constitutes an adequate diet.
c. Takes interest in attractiveness and appropriateness of patient's trays; assists with making corrections promptly.
d. Provides pleasant atmosphere for mealtime; wherever possible, provides company — other patients, volunteers, visitors.

39. **Recognizes and Reports Behavioral and Physiologic Changes That Are Due to Drugs.**
a. Takes appropriate action and reports skin reactions of patients receiving drugs.
b. Watches for photosensitivity, limiting exposure to sun.
c. Talks with patients to determine if they are aware of changes.

40. **Adjusts Expectations of Patient's Behavior According to the Effect the Drug Has on the Patient.**
a. Accepts drowsiness and retarded psychomotor activity by supporting the patient when he points out that he is unable to participate in active discussions or sports.
b. Finds projects for the tremulous patient that require little coordination.
c. Provides rest periods for patients indicating that they are too tired to participate in daily routine.

41. **Demonstrates Understanding of Both Medical and Surgical Asepsis.**
a. Recognizes breaks in techniques and takes steps to correct them.
b. Washes hands as necessary; e.g., on completing care of one patient and before moving to another, before beginning "clean" procedure, following any obvious contamination, etc.
c. Recognizes floor as area of gross contamination; e.g., cleanses or replaces items picked up from floor; washes hands after picking something up from the floor; avoids placing supplies or equipment on the floor.
d. Reviews means of transmission of particular disease when patient is admitted with or develops a communicable disease, and plans techniques to avoid dissemination of particular organisms, without complicating process by carrying out ritualistic precautions unrelated to paths of transmission of organisms.
e. Handles dressing so that surface that will cover wound and surrounding area remains sterile.

42. **Recognizes Hazards to Patient Safety and Takes Appropriate Action to Maintain a Safe Environment and to Give Patient Feeling of Being Safe.**
a. Ensures assistance of sufficient number of persons when a patient is to be lifted — to ensure safety and feeling of safety for the patient; to ensure no strain for the patient or the personnel.

b. Provides side rails for all older patients during first few days in hospital. Discusses their use with the patient; provides side rails for restless or disoriented patients.

c. Notes placement of various cords and tubing: ensures that they will not be tripped over or accidentally jerked out of place.

d. Discusses reasons for No Smoking signs in presence of oxygen administration with patient and visitors.

43. **Carries Out Safety Measures Developed to Prevent Patients from Harming Themselves or Others.**

a. Reports threats made by patients to harm themselves or others.

b. Makes sure transportation equipment is safe; labels it unsafe if repairs are needed and secures safe equipment rather than taking any risk.

c. Stays with patients whose behavior indicates impulsiveness and confusion.

d. Asks for help when needed to provide safety for the patient himself and/or personnel.

44. **Carries Out Established Technique for Safe Administration of Medications and Parenteral Fluids.**

a. Checks medication card against written orders the first time particular medication is administered to particular patient on particular day.

b. Checks container label three times; if interrupted during preparation, repeats the three-time check.

c. Addresses patient by name before giving the medication.

d. Administers only medications she herself has prepared.

GENERAL

Actions that may be directed toward meeting either psychosocial or physical needs of patients, or both at the same time.

45. **Utilizes Patient Teaching Opportunities.**

a. Encourages new mother to ask questions about care of herself and new baby during first weeks at home. Guides mother as she picks up baby, demonstrates and has mother demonstrate holding baby for burping and bathing.

b. Discusses patient's plans for work after he leaves the hospital, tells him of agencies that will provide people to help him find training and employment opportunities.

c. Discusses medications patient will be taking at home; ensures that he knows identity of each, purpose for which it is being prescribed, dosage and schedule, and expected effects of medication.

d. Initiates discussion about illness, treatment, and plans for care, rather than waiting for patient to ask questions; uses questions to determine what patient knows and understands.

46. **Involves Patient and Family in Planning for Care and Treatments.**
   a. When giving instructions to patient, involves family member if he is visiting — not only allowing him to remain in the room, but actually including him in discussion.
   b. Encourages family member to observe treatments, especially those that may be expected to be carried on at home.
   c. Arranges to have family member participate in treatments, eventually doing entire treatment, if it is one patient will not be able to do himself.
   d. Plans with patient and family members to do care procedures at time when family member can participate; plans details of care to be needed at home with patient and family members.
   e. Helps patient communicate with family about needs for items and procedures of care after discharge; e.g., wife to know diet, husband to know of work-saving methods and devices, parents to anticipate teasing of child by other children and ways to help child cope.

47. **Protects Sensitivities of the Patient.**
   a. Uses sheets or towels as drapes to avoid unnecessary exposure of body.
   b. Draws curtain around bed for all procedures of physical care.
   c. Arranges to have patient taken to room where interview (social worker, psychologist, homemaker) can be conducted in private.
   d. Allows patient to complete own bath or seeks assistance from person of same sex; leaves room during procedure if indicated; leaves room during portions of physical examination should patient desire this; is particularly alert to sensitivities of maturing child and teenager.

48. **Encourages Patient to Accept Dependence/Independence as Appropriate to His Condition.**
   a. Discusses role of rest in treatment of heart disease; reassures patient of gradual progress toward resumption of responsibility of doing for himself.
   b. Helps patient with extensive surgery to understand the mechanisms involved in various elements of early ambulation and the purposes to be served by doing his exercises and daily care tasks.
   c. Helps patient with extensive disability of skeletal-muscular system to understand involvement, rationale for prescribed treatments, progress to be anticipated, timing to be anticipated in relation to various degrees of recovery, and degree of recovery to be expected in relation to degree of effort expended by patient.

    d. Helps patient understand appropriateness of dependent role, reassures him that he will be helped to resume independence as soon as it is good for him to do so.

49. **Utilizes Resources Within the Milieu to Provide Patient with Opportunities for Problem Solving.**
    a. Encourages patient to suggest ways to accomplish "routine" tasks despite limitation due to incapacitated or absent body feature. Helps him plan placement of articles as he will use them in hospital and at home or work.
    b. Helps patient consider alternatives in relation to choice of evening's entertainment; e.g., baseball game, long-awaited movie, visit of mother-in-law.
    c. Helps child to select toy, to understand implication of selection; e.g., kind of toy or game that can be used in bed, one that may allow only for solitary play, or one that will allow others to join in play, etc.
    d. Asks patients to propose furniture arrangement that will provide for best use of day and artificial lighting and for least distressful light glares.

50. **Allows Patient Freedom of Choice in Details of Daily Living Whenever Possible and Within Patient's Ability to Make Choice.**
    a. Determines whether patient is "early" or "late" riser, plans with him about timing for needed care.
    b. Allows patient morning or evening shower or bath depending on custom and preference.
    c. Assists patient to arrange for type of clothing he prefers to wear.
    d. Grants requests involving changes in daily routines that can be made without major disruptions in ward plans.

51. **Encourages Patient to Take Part in Activities of Daily Living That Will Stimulate His Potential for Positive Growth**
    a. Encourages "early" riser to assist with serving morning coffee, where it is a practice.
    b. Encourages stroke patient to shave himself, provides electric razor if indicated.
    c. Invites patient to assist with caring for flowers — his own and those of others.
    d. Encourages patient to utilize problem-solving approach when dealing with problems involving activities of daily living.
    e. Gives recognition for patient's efforts and successes.

52. **Adapts Activities to Physical and Mental Abilities of Patients.**
    a. Ensures that patient understands care procedure in which he is to be involved and what is expected of him; e.g., explaining (1) first few colos-

tomy dressing changes, (2) tracheostomy suctioning, (3) hip spica cast removal, (4) intramuscular injection.

b. Guides confused patient through steps of preparation for visit to therapist: reminds patient, one step at a time, about washing face and hands, brushing teeth, combing hair, dressing, storing night clothing, etc.

c. Allows time for small child or slow or hesitant patient to do things for himself, so that he may develop confidence and independence.

d. Provides assistance to patient before he reaches point of frustration at inability to perform task.

53. **Adapts Nursing Care to Patient's Level and Pace of Development.**

a. Allows child to perform tasks of which he is capable; provides him with challenge to learn new tasks that are within his ability to learn and perform.

b. Avoids "contests" related to learning new tasks, where differences between patients' potential to learn or perform are obviously such that some patients would experience frustration and feelings of inadequacy.

c. Repeats instructions and allows patient to attempt repeated performances, offering needed suggestion and assistance.

d. Allows patient to change his mind; assists patient to rethink a problem and decide to pursue a path different from one selected earlier. If indicated, assists patient to reassure himself that original choice was correct one.

54. **Provides for Diversional and Treatment Activities Appropriate to Patient's Capabilities and Needs.**

a. Sings to small children at bedtime.

b. Has no more than three adolescents working on one jigsaw puzzle at one time.

c. Provides bedside commode for patient unable to walk to bathroom.

d. Takes older patients to dayroom and spends time with them, encouraging them to visit or share activity; e.g., needlework, cards, sports on TV (*not* TV soap operas).

55. **Allows for Slow or Unskilled Performance Without Showing Annoyance or Impatience.**

a. Uses gentle persuasion to keep regressed patient moving in process of morning toilet and dressing.

b. Assists aphasic patient to say words rather than saying them for him.

c. Encourages patient learning to take his own blood pressure with words of reassurance and proposal that he try again.

d. Waits for emphysema patient to catch breath after rising to sit on edge of bed and before helping him to walk to chair.

56. **Establishes Nursing Care Goals Within the Framework of the Therapist's Plan of Care.**
    a. Relates nursing goals to the therapist's goals.
    b. Assists new mother with breast feeding.
    c. Removes child's tray after thirty minutes, regardless of amount of food eaten (when purpose is to assist child to establish habit of eating and not playing with food).
    d. Plans toileting schedule with paraplegic patient, with view to achieving independence from indwelling catheter.

57. **Adapts to and Works with Varied Approaches to Treatment.**
    a. Helps patient and personnel understand reason for cast, when patient in next bed is in traction for seemingly the same type of cervical spine injury.
    b. Uses sugar and aeroplast spray for one patient's decubitus and aeroplast spray alone for another.
    c. Participates with others in providing care that is consistent and in agreement with recommended approach.
    d. Encourages one patient to talk of death and dying, avoids or changes subject with another.

58. **Relates to Patient Within the Framework of the Therapeutic Plan.**
    a. Supports the therapeutic goal to reality, orients the patient by pointing out reality when patient appears confused.
    b. Reassures patient that coming in to check blood pressure every fifteen minutes is not too much trouble.
    c. Reassures patient learning to use crutches that she will remain near and will support him if needed, but encourages him to try to walk with only support of crutches.
    d. Develops plan to make a "game" of process of helping aphasic patient relearn handling of words.

59. **Watchfulness Is Carried Out in an Unobtrusive Manner.**
    a. Moves quietly into and out of room when frequent checking is required; e.g., IV or O_2 flow, pulse, blood pressure, etc.
    b. Is gentle when removing bedclothing for repeated checking for bleeding; when pressing tissues to test distension, edema, or circulation in limb in a cast; when preparing to give IM injection.
    c. Approaches and stands quietly beside group engaged in game or conversation without interrupting or distracting attention of members of group.
    d. Participates with patients known to be impulsive to facilitate observation and protection.

60. **Responds Appropriately to Emergency Situations.**
   a. Waits until help is available to move patient who has fallen from bed.
   b. Speaks quietly to patient who has assumed posture to suit his words of threatening to strike her.
   c. Remains with patient who is choking or gasping for breath.
   d. Prepares stimulants for administration in anticipation of physician's orders for patient with cardiac arrest.

COMMUNICATION

Communication on behalf of patients.

61. **Communicates Ideas, Facts, Feelings, and Concepts Clearly in Speech.**
   a. Gives complete description of patient's behavior, using good sequence and without excessive repetition.
   b. Expresses feelings in normal tone, without either mumbling or high emotionalism.
   c. Reports observations objectively, without resorting to meaningless generalizations.
   d. Uses questions to help aides report and describe patient's condition and to ascertain that aides have understood plan for care.

62. **Communicates Ideas, Facts, Feelings, and Concepts Clearly in Writing.**
   a. Charts precise and specific observations; uses few generalizing clichés.
   b. Records possible interpretation of reason for patient's behavior.
   c. Uses nouns; avoids using pronouns that could lead to misinterpretations or misidentifications.

63. **Establishes a Well-Developed Nursing Care Plan.**
   a. Includes immediate and long-range objectives of care.
   b. Includes information about patient's likes and dislikes.
   c. Includes suggestions for modification of procedures that make care easier or more effective for patient.
   d. Includes plan for progressive care in relation to anticipated future needs of patient; e.g., "plan to teach colon irrigation beginning tomorrow."

64. **Gives Accurate Reports, Verbal and Written, of Patient Behavior, Including Behavior That Involved Interaction with Self.**
   a. Reports that patient refused to take IM injection, claiming she hurt him last time she gave it.
   b. Reports patient's refusal to sit up in chair; patient states she left him up too long yesterday.
   c. Includes her responses during the interaction with the patient.

65. **Participates Freely in Ward Patient-Care Conferences.**
    a. Volunteers observations she has made.
    b. Supplies information about a particular disease condition and recommended treatment.
    c. Offers proposals of approaches to care of particular patient.
    d. Asks questions that will elicit information or ideas from other workers.

66. **Communicates Effectively and Establishes Good Relationships with Other Disciplines.**
    a. Consults with physical therapist about "physio" treatment of patient, seeking suggestions of what nurses might do to enhance treatment.
    b. Calls social worker to suggest that a patient might benefit from help, volunteering information about patient and family.
    c. Notifies X-ray or lab, as indicated, to clarify orders for preparation of patient or when patient will be delayed or unable to keep appointment.
    d. Makes certain that physician learns all pertinent information about patient; reports verbally, places bold print note on front of chart, requests that head nurse inform physician.

67. **Attends to Patient's Needs Through Use of Referrals, Both to Departments in the Hospital as Agency and to Other Community Agencies.**
    a. Requests occupational therapy consultation for patient with severely injured hand.
    b. Makes VNA referral for new mother with first baby who is new to city and has no family or friends who can assist with teaching care of new baby.
    c. Consults with social worker about referral to visiting housekeeper for elderly patient who lives alone.
    d. Calls local school system to arrange for home teaching for adolescent patient.

PROFESSIONAL IMPLICATIONS

Actions directed toward fulfilling responsibilities of a nurse in all facets and varieties of patient care situations.

68. **Is Self-Directing: Takes Initiative and Goes Ahead on Own.**
    a. Provides side rails for elderly patient who has been admitted for injuries following a fall; discusses reason for rails with the patient.
    b. Notices patient in chair seems tired, seeks assistance and helps patient back to bed.
    c. Notices IV is infiltrating tissues; stops flow and notifies physician.
    d. Asks questions when in doubt regarding treatment goals and utilizes knowledge and facilities to meet goals.

69. **Makes Decisions Willingly and Appropriately.**
  a. Phones supervisor (in absence of charge nurse) to report staffing that could endanger patient safety; reports requirements for patient care, present plan for caring for patients, and anticipated effects of limited staff.
  b. Suggests that two persons care for certain patient whenever he must be moved, with view to promoting patient safety, feeling of safety, and comfort, reducing time, and moving to achieve positioning in good body alignment.
  c. Changes lunchtime for aide to permit him to accompany patient to cystoscopy.
  d. Calls physician when patient "jokingly" comments that he thinks he will not have his operation the next morning, but will perhaps jump out the window instead.

70. **Makes Decisions That Reflect Both Knowledge of Facts and Good Judgment.**
  a. Changes room assignment of patient whose baby died during delivery to avoid placing her in room with mother with day-old baby.
  b. Administers both PRN analgesic and PRN hypnotic at bedtime to second-day postoperative patient with spinal fusion.
  c. Promptly slows flow of IV when she notices postoperative patient manifesting increased difficulty in and rate of breathing.
  d. Suggests that emphysema patient be served six small feedings a day.

71. **Gives Verbal Evidence of Good Insight into Deeper Problems and Needs of Patients.**
  a. Proposes that patient who lost first two children at birth not be left alone any more than necessary, that nurses "be with her" and share her experience with her.
  b. Suggests ways that personnel might help adolescent with severe acne to recognize and utilize assets and abilities to contribute to interest and happiness of others, thereby gaining confidence and satisfaction in his own worth.
  c. Is sincere when speculating regarding the possible dynamics of behavior and provides supportive evidence.

72. **Contributes as Nurse Member of Health Team to Planning and Evaluating Care.**
  a. Reports care with which patient will need help at home and suggests persons in home who might provide the help.
  b. Suggests that wound be dressed following wife's visit, since dressing upsets patient and he discusses little else with her and sometimes will not speak at all.

c. Suggests that patient willingly performs arm exercises, but seldom does leg exercises when therapist is not present.

73. **Spends Time with Patients, Rather Than with Other Nurses or Hospital Personnel.**
    a. Identifies and performs "extra" tasks with patients, as time permits; e.g.:
       (1) Encourages colostomy patient to discuss plans for care when he goes home and returns to work.
       (2) Discusses return to school plans with adolescent who has missed final four months of twelfth grade, due to motorcycle accident.
       (3) Gets patient out of bed.
       (4) Renews plastic and adhesive on edges of body cast.
    b. Leaves "visiting" session of ward personnel to visit with patients.
    c. Leads nurse-to-nurse conversation to include patients and to focus on patients interests.

74. **Reliable: Follows Through with Responsibilities.**
    a. Asks for help in doubtful situations, rather than making errors.
    b. Reports when work is not completed.
    c. Views situation herself, rather than depending on reports alone; e.g., visits patient on report of bleeding, checks conditions of very ill patients in preparation for change-of-shift report.
    d. Periodically reviews assignment and work accomplished with view to re-planning and establishing priorities and fulfilling responsibilities for all of day's assignments.

75. **Stays with Assigned Patients, or Knows Where and How They Are.**
    a. Visits all assigned patients to ascertain their conditions before beginning tasks of the day.
    b. Knows where patients are, reasons for their being off the ward or away from bedside unit, and when they are expected to return.
    c. Knows current condition, as well as changes in past 24 hours, of all assigned patients, and can report plans for care of each.

76. **Impresses Others with Sincerity of Interest and Nursing Effort.**
    a. Offers constructive suggestions for improvements in care of individual patients and in routines on nursing unit.
    b. Undertakes additional tasks when her own assignments are completed.
    c. Tries new ways of doing things — those suggested by others and those devised by herself.

77. **Gives Continued Interest and Encouragement to Various-Level Programs, Whether Directed to Care of Patients of Her Immediate Concern or Institution-Wide Programs.**
    a. Assists with evaluation of programs; e.g., conscientiously makes and records formalized observations, reports casual observations, suggests interpretations of apparent results of programs.
    b. Helps interpret new administrative policies and offers suggestions for implementing procedures needed to carry out policies; e.g., proposes appropriate role of nurse in new patient-billing plan, helps with planning for husbands to be with wives during labor and for fathers' classes, discusses new rotation plan with aides.
    c. Encourages and supports mothers in breast feeding.
    d. Identifies patients who will need professional nursing care after discharge, in nursing home or own home.

78. **Participates in Staff Meetings.**
    a. Reports innovation on own nursing unit that might be useful on other units.
    b. Reports ideas from current literature that may have meaning for functioning of her own nursing service.
    c. Asks pertinent questions.
    d. Suggests programs or persons that might provide staff with information and ideas for improvements in practice.
    e. Volunteers for committee membership.

79. **Avails Self of Opportunities for Learning.**
    a. Discusses patient's condition and rationale of treatment with physician and paramedical specialists.
    b. Uses ward library to learn about diseases and treatments of particular patients.
    c. Asks for additional explanation to enhance her knowledge and understanding of patients' conditions and treatments.
    d. Plans work so she can attend therapy conferences or film sessions.

80. **Is a Good Follower (Helpful, Cooperative).**
    a. Willingly performs tasks assigned to her.
    b. Accepts less than desirable assignments.
    c. Offers to help others, makes point of ensuring that new staff member feels free to seek help or ask about unfamiliar things.
    d. Offers suggestions for movement toward team goals without usurping prerogative of leader.

e. Accepts rejection of her suggestions and readily moves to follow plan established by group or by leader.

81. **Is a Good Leader (Constructive).**
   a. Invites suggestions from members of group.
   b. Gives recognition to achievement of individual members and to that of group as a whole.
   c. Offers instruction and guidance when proposing a different way of doing things.
   d. Encourages members of group to express likes and dislikes and to choose portion of work they would like to do.
   e. Assists group to evaluate work accomplished and plan continued work.

82. **Is Helpful to Ward Personnel.**
   a. Discusses rationale for patient care, helping personnel to know why treatments are prescribed in relation to patient's illness and expected effects of treatments.
   b. Ascertains knowledge personnel have about new or different or unusual "case"; teaches or plans ways that all can increase their knowledge.
   c. At mid-shift, determines progress with work and offers assistance with planning for or accomplishing completion.
   d. Assists with planning modification of treatment or procedure when patient's condition or cast or traction necessitate innovation.

83. **Cooperates with Ward Routines and Hospital Regulations.**
   a. Assists with children's toileting and handwashing before meals.
   b. Plans own schedule in consultation with others so that she will prepare for her patients at a time when others will not be doing theirs.
   c. Performs treatments at times that will not interfere with visiting hours.
   d. Courteously explains to visitors reasons for not allowing patients to have food brought in and left at bedside.

84. **Accepts Authority Situations with Understanding.**
   a. Willingly moves to another nursing unit to fill emergency vacancy.
   b. Accepts fact that two year-end holidays cannot be taken together and in combination with a weekend.
   c. Refuses, politely but firmly, to carry out physician order that is in opposition to hospital policy; e.g., IV medication, adding second bottle of blood without physician present, phone order for narcotic, too old narcotic order, suture removal, etc.
   d. Accepts and carries out the recommendations of people in supervisory positions.

Instructions for Use
of the Scale

FORMAT OF THE SCALE

The format of the Scale is essentially self-explanatory.

To allow ready identification of a particular column, parentheses are provided for recording ratings in the Best, Average, and Poorest Staff Nurse columns, and horizontal rules are used for the other columns.

THE YARDSTICK

The yardstick or standard against which observed nursing care actions will be measured to determine the score for individual observations is the "quality of care (performance) expected of a first-level staff nurse."

The magnitude of the scale is the competence expected of a "Best" Staff Nurse. The scale is divided into five subunits, identified as levels of competence ranging from "Poorest" through "Average" to "Best" Staff Nurse.

Each rater develops her own individual frame of reference to serve as a concrete yardstick against which to measure competence displayed by a nurse performing nursing care activities.

INDIVIDUAL FRAME OF REFERENCE

An individual frame of reference is developed by each rater according to the instructions on the form below. This frame of reference may then be used as her yardstick whenever she rates actions performed by a person providing care to patients. Should settings change markedly, such as from a geriatric nursing unit to a well-baby clinic, the rater may want to change the names of the staff nurses on her form to names of nurses she recalls working in the particular specialized setting, but the general process of developing and applying the frame of reference remains the same.

GENERAL FRAME OF REFERENCE

Some persons may prefer to use a more general frame of reference for their yardstick and its subunits. Testing has demonstrated that raters discriminate adequately among individuals and among various nursing actions when they use the generalized five-point scale with the somewhat abstract point identifications: Excellent, Above Average, Average, Below Average, and Poor. Others have suggested the descriptions: Most Comprehensive Care, Between, Average, Between, and Most Limited Care. Findings from tests of the Slater Scale and from studies by others using a Likert-type scale reveal that variations in adjectives which hold generally common meanings for raters do not yield differences in ratings. The adjectives suggested here, along with an individual frame of reference based on known nurses, provide for a more concrete frame of reference than do the general adjectives. Furthermore, they serve more definitively as reminders of the standard of measurement – the performance expected of a first-level staff nurse.

INDIVIDUAL FRAME OF REFERENCE FORM

for development and use of
the standard of measurement:

PERFORMANCE EXPECTED OF A FIRST-LEVEL STAFF NURSE

Write the names of staff nurses whom you know or have known in the respective boxes:

1. Write the name of the nurse whom you consider to be the best staff nurse you have known (the nurse you would like to have care for you, should you be ill) in the box labeled "Best Staff Nurse."
2. Think of the nurse you consider to be the poorest staff nurse you have ever known; write her name in the box on the far right, labeled "Poorest Staff Nurse."
3. Think of a nurse whom you consider to be a typical or average staff nurse, neither noticeably good nor noticeably poor; write her name in the middle box, labeled "Average Staff Nurse."
4. Think of a nurse who falls between your "best" and your "average" nurse and one who falls between your "average" nurse and your "poorest" nurse; write their names in the respective boxes.

Best Staff Nurse	Between	Average Staff Nurse	Between	Poorest Staff Nurse
_____	_____	_____	_____	_____
_____	_____	_____	_____	_____
0 – +	0 – +	0 – +	0 – +	0
BEST		AVERAGE		POOREST

USING THE SCALE WITH A FIVE-POINT YARDSTICK

The nursing care actions (items) listed on the Scale are of a low order of abstraction, and the cues provided in the accompanying Cue Sheet are suggested observable behaviors that may be rated to score any particular item.

1. Consider the actions of the nurse being rated (ratee) in relation to each item on the Scale.
2. Judge the competency displayed by the nurse, comparing her performance to that of nurses identified in the individual frame of reference.

3. Decide which of the staff nurses the subject most resembles in performing actions that are representative of the item.
4. Place a check or rating symbol in the column corresponding to the selected (reference) nurse.

OBSERVATIONS AND RETROSPECTIVE RATINGS

5. Use nurse actions listed in the Cue Sheet and anecdotal notes to help recall observations of interactions with or interventions on behalf of patients by the person being rated, which will allow rating a particular item.
6. Single or multiple rating of an item:
    a. Ratings may be done for each episode recalled that allows rating of two or more scale items. This will yield many and varied measurements for each item.
    b. As the rater considers rating an individual item, she may do a mental calculation of the level of performance of various episodes and ascribe a single rating to represent the ratee's general level of performance of actions germane to the item being rated.
    c. One episode of care may allow ratings on several items; rather than choosing a single one to be rated, it is best to score all pertinent items.

At first, the rater will find herself moving back and forth in focusing on the item to be rated and on an episode that allows the rating of one or more items. As she becomes accustomed to using the scale, she will focus on the items in sequence, with repeated recall of individual episodes that permit rating various individual items. This is in contrast to focusing on a single episode and skipping to those items for which it provides ratings, as will be done in on-the-spot observations and ratings, described below.

ON-THE-SPOT OBSERVATIONS AND RATINGS

1. Listen to change-of-shift reports on patients for whom the ratee will be providing care.
2. Become just as familiar with the patients as if the rater were to be providing care for the ratee's patients.
3. Shadow the ratee for two and one-half to three hours.
4. Rate all items germane to each episode of nursing care performed by the ratee. Here focus will be on the episode; several items related to a given episode will be rated before a following episode is considered.
5. Take notes if desired to promote recall of episodes so that other items may later be rated when there is time to do them.
6. Do not necessarily rate all items that an episode might warrant. Raters have found that they usually rate from five to six items per episode before moving on to rate the next episode.
7. Rate each item for each episode which provides for such rating, whether individual ratings are the same or different from prior ratings for the same item.

8. When the shadowing time is completed:
   a. Review the items and, on the basis of notes and recall, add ratings for items not already scored and additional ones for items with earlier ratings.
   b. Check the Not Observed and Not Applicable items.

NOT OBSERVED AND NOT APPLICABLE ITEMS

1. Check an item "not observed" when the rater has not observed nursing care actions that would have allowed rating the item, although such actions would have been possible, appropriate, and expected in the settings in which the ratee had been providing care to patients.
2. Check an item "not applicable" when the situation in which the ratee was providing care was such that opportunity for performance of nursing care actions that permit rating the item was unlikely. For example, were the ratee caring for premature infants, she would not be expected to engage in actions encompassed in item 16, "Chooses Appropriate Topics for Conversation."

Neither the Not Observed nor the Not Applicable column is likely to be used frequently in retrospective ratings, since in such a case the ratee would have been observed over a period of time, during which many and varied types of nursing care situations would have occurred, providing opportunity for performance of a wide range of nursing care actions.

OMITTED OR INAPPROPRIATE NURSING CARE ACTIONS

1. Where the ratee fails to perform nursing care actions that should be performed, given the patients' needs and conditions, the appropriate measurement is Poorest Nurse; the action would not be checked as Not Observed.
2. Similarly, the Not Applicable column should not be used to rate actions that are inappropriate to patients' needs or conditions; such care would be rated in the Poorest Nurse column.

The Not Applicable device is the feature that makes the Slater Scale usable in any setting in which nurse-patient interactions occur. Should the setting in which a ratee is working not provide opportunity for performing actions that would allow measurements identified in some of the items, such individual measurements can be omitted from the total set of measurements used to calculate the final score without seriously affecting the determination of the level of competence displayed by the ratee. This is true even in a situation where no nursing care actions are apt to be required in a particular area of nursing function, such as the area of Psychosocial: Group. It is still possible to rate the minimum number of 60 items, and a reliable evaluation score of nursing competence can be calculated.

The rater is cautioned not to ascribe nonapplicability to particular items of care too readily. It is generally thought that items in functional area II, Psychosocial: Group, apply only in psychiatric settings; yet, they are pertinent in pediatrics, geriatrics, out-patient care, and other settings as well.

CUE SHEET*

What Are the Cues?

1. Concrete examples of interactions/interventions by nurse with or in behalf of patients which are illustrations of the items.
2. Arbitrarily selected examples of actions that permit ascribing a rating to one or more items.
3. Descriptions of interactions/interventions derived from various health care settings.

Why Have Cues?

1. Cues identify nurse-patient interactions on a level even more concrete than the items.
2. Cues serve as reminders of kinds of activities that permit ratings of one or more items.
3. Cues facilitate orientation of the rater to the scale.
4. Cues promote the flexibility and scope of application for the scale, through reminders of actions from various care settings and by permitting users to add or modify cues to suit particular situations in which the scale is to be used.

How to Use Cues

1. Ascribe rating to item of which cue is an illustration; do not rate the cue itself.
2. Review cues before and during rating sessions for reminders of:
   a. activities that permit ascribing ratings;
   b. items to be rated on the basis of particular activities.
3. Delete, add, or modify cues to suit particular situation in which Scale is to be used; e.g., for a maternity care setting or an ambulatory care setting.
4. Delete, add, or modify cues to update scale.
5. Ratings should *not* be limited to interactions listed in the cue sheet but should be ascribed to any nursing actions performed or omitted, with or on behalf of patients, that are pertinent to meeting nursing care needs.

*The section on cues is taken from *Quality Patient Care Scale* (New York: Appleton-Century-Crofts, 1974), which uses the same device.

6. For each interaction, ratings should be ascribed to as many items as the rater finds to be represented by it.
7. Cues will be used most often during orientation to the Scale and for reorientation following a period of not using the Scale.

The Cue Sheet is another feature of the Slater Scale that enhances its usability in all settings where nurse-patient interactions occur. As now constructed, cues for any one item are examples of nurse actions in two or more clinical settings. No item on the Scale may be changed without sacrificing the value of the testing that confirms the value of the Scale as a measuring instrument. Nonetheless, the cues may be modified in any manner desired – by editing, by addition, and by deletion – so that users may provide a set of cues directly applicable to the setting in which the nurses to be rated are working. They may eliminate reminders that do not apply in their setting, those that serve more to distract than to bring to recall.

Two features, the Not Applicable column and the opportunity of changing the cue sheets, eliminate the need to develop specific tools for specific nursing care settings. The tool can be adapted to specific settings and particular clinical practice through use of these two mechanisms.

USING THE SCALE WITH A THIRTEEN-POINT YARDSTICK

1. The frame of reference is identical to that used with the five-point yardstick, and the same process is followed until the reference nurse is identified.
2. When the reference nurse has been identified, the rater decides whether the ratee performs in a manner identical to the reference nurse, a bit better than the reference nurse, or a bit poorer.
3. If the performance is judged to be exactly like that of the reference nurse, a zero will be placed in the appropriate box opposite the item on the scale. If the performance is better than that of the reference nurse, a plus (+) will be placed in the box; if poorer, the recorded symbol will be a minus (−).

The symbols are shown below each reference nurse's name box on the Frame of Reference Form. There is no plus for the Best Staff Nurse, since a subject would not be expected to perform better than the best; likewise, there is no minus for the Poorest Staff Nurse.

The device of identifying the reference nurse and then measuring the performance of the ratee as just like, better than, or poorer than that of the reference nurse provides a yardstick with thirteen subunits, instead of the more commonly used five subunits. Yet, in effect, the rater is required only to make judgments on the five-unit scale and then on a three-unit scale.

This device is recommended when repeated measurements of a single subject are necessary over a brief period of time, such as an evaluation every two weeks of a twelve-week learning period. It provides for a finer measurement than the five-point scale, yet it does not require the rater to make a judgment on more than five- and three-point scales.

CALCULATING THE EVALUATION SCORE

1. The numerical values for the levels of performance range from 5 to 1, with Best Nurse equal to 5.
2. The score is derived by totaling the scores of all items rated and dividing by the number of items rated (carrying to one decimal point).
3. Not Observed and Not Applicable items are omitted in calculating the score.
4. When single ratings are ascribed to each item rated, summing of the rating scores is straightforward.
5. When multiple ratings are ascribed to an item, a mean score should be calculated by adding the scores of the ratings and dividing by the number of ratings of the item (carried to one decimal point). This mean will then be the score used in summing the scores of all items rated. In other words, the evaluation score may be a mean of the scores for all rated items, or the mean of the mean scores of all rated items.
6. Calculation of the evaluation score should be done as a separate step, following completion of the ratings; this task may be performed by a clerk.
7. Ratings of 60 of the 84 items are sufficient to provide a valid and reliable evaluation score for the ratee. Extensive use of the Scale has shown that, regardless of the clinical setting, raters are able to score 75 or more items in retrospective ratings. For on-the-spot ratings, it has been possible to make sufficient observations to allow rating of 60 or more items during two and one-half to three hours of continuous observation.
8. For the 13-point scale, the scoring is similar, but the numerical values will range from 13 to 1, with the zero rating in the Best Nurse column scored as 13, the minus in the Best Nurse column as 12, and so on, down to 1 for the zero in the Poorest Nurse column.
9. If desired, other scores may be ascribed; for example, 65 to 5, after the scaling used in the Syracuse Scales of Social Relations (Gardner and Thompson), from which the basic idea of the 13-point scale is derived.

In relation to the term "evaluation score," in contrast to scores for individual item ratings, the reader is reminded of one definition of evaluation that is particularly apt here: Evaluation may be thought of as a generalization that describes a judgment based on many measurements.

ORIENTATION TO USE OF THE SLATER SCALE

The rater should spend some time familiarizing herself with the Scale, the cues, the guides for use, and background discussions in the section: Standard of Measurement and the Ratings. She should then attempt a retrospective evaluation of a nurse whose work she has observed. Persons report that they spend any-where from two and one-half to four hours doing this first evaluation, with the most frequent time being three to three and one-half hours. That is perhaps all that should be done during the first orientation tryout.

For the second try, all that is needed is an overview of guides for use and a review of cues, followed by a second retrospective rating. The second rating may be expected to require about two hours.

The rater is now ready to do ratings "for real."

All orientation materials should be read thoroughly for a second time. The rater will find that, by the time she has done ratings on four subjects, she will complete retrospective ratings in 30 to 40 minutes.

Standard of Measurement and the Ratings

PROLOGUE: SUBJECTIVITY AND JUDGMENT

A difficulty frequently identified by persons considering the use of tools for evaluating the clinical competence of nurses is the problem of subjectivity in measurement. In a way, it seems remarkable that nurses should feel so much discomfort about the matter of subjectivity and "subjective judgment" in the evaluation of nurses' clinical competence. This is particularly so for clinical instructors and supervisors. Their whole effort in clinical instruction, guidance, and supervision is aimed toward assisting nurses to make judgments. The professional nurse's forte is her clinical judgment. In all her clinical supervision, the instructor or supervisor uses her own clinical judgment to determine when a nurse under supervision is making a correct judgment and when she may need guidance to improve her judgment. This is accepted — no problem. But let the supervisor redirect her conscious focus away from guidance and instruction and toward evaluation of the nurse's display of clinical competence — a large part of which is professional judgment — and she and all about her question the validity of the evaluation she might make, because it is based on subjective judgment! Her use of clinical judgment is accepted without question when she uses it to instruct. But when she uses it to evaluate the result of her instruction, it immediately becomes less than satisfactory (Wandelt, 1973).

THE RATINGS: OBJECTIVITY AND SUBJECTIVITY

There is always a quest for objective evaluation and the elimination of subjective judgment. The imprecise use of terms leads to redundancy in the expression "subjective judgment," and to antithesis in the expression "objective evaluation." Perhaps it would be helpful to consider precisely what these words mean:

To judge is to form an idea or an opinion about; to think or suppose.

Subjective means of, affected by, or produced by the mind.

Objective means of or having to do with a material object as distinguished from a mental concept, ideal, or belief; based on observable phenomena; presented factually.

Measurement is a comparison of a single phenomenon with a standard of measurement; the recorded number or symbol that represents the magnitude of the phenomenon in terms of the magnitude of the standard of measurement.

All judgment includes both objective and subjective components. Professional judgments are based on facts, but the facts lead to actions only when the catalyst of subjectivity is brought into play.

All measurements of nursing actions involve judgments, and, in turn, the evaluations are judgments based on measurements of the nursing actions.

COMPETENCE AND PERFORMANCE

To understand the elements of objectivity and subjectivity inherent in all measurement and evaluatory judgments of clinical competence, it is helpful to consider the distinction between mere performance of nursing care actions and the competence displayed in the performance of the actions. Many actions performed may be repetitious and identical, regardless of circumstances or setting. The performance of actions that results from competence, however, conceivably may never be the same on any two occasions. Inherent in the concept of competence are elements of problem-solving ability, ability to perform so as to achieve an objective in situations never before encountered and with materials never before used (Brunner).

When the idea of nursing care is generalized to care being provided to patients, thinking may be in terms of skilled performance of nursing care actions.

When the idea of nursing care is narrowed to care being provided to an individual patient, thinking focuses on manifestations of competence in adapting actions to suit the patient's unique needs and the immediate circumstances in which the care is being given. The Slater Scale was developed to provide measurements of the competence of a nurse in utilizing and adapting skilled performance to unique needs and circumstances of care. It is because the quality of the performance of a nurse must be judged in relation to her competence to accommodate to unique situations that the person doing the measurement must be capable of making judgments about the quality of the performance in relation to the many aspects of the circumstances in which the actions are performed. What is condemned as subjective, with the connotation of personal opinion biased by personality and other psychological considerations, may not and need not be that at all. Rather, the subjective elements in a judgment may well be knowledge from sciences and previous experience, along with decisions about needs *of the patient* The rater synthesizes her own knowledge and the objective observations in the immediate situation to derive the measurement of the level of competence manifested in the performance of a particular action in a particular situation.

THE JUDGMENT/RATING PROCESS

As a rater observes a nurse-patient interaction, she will note the care component of the interaction, and she will consider the needs of the patient — his total needs, overall, long range, and immediate. She will compare the care components of the interaction with the care expected of a first-level staff nurse; she will make a judgment of the quality of the interaction's contribution to meeting the patient's needs.

She will consider the content of the action and the tone of the action as performed and conveyed by the nurse. She will make a judgment about the quality of the nurse's performance and record her judgment in the appropriate column in the scale.

Because of the many personal and situational elements involved in any nurse-patient interaction, it is impossible to construct an instrument that will provide for strictly objective measurement of the quality of the interaction or of any aspect of it. The best that can be hoped for is a measuring device that helps the rater to focus on a single interaction and to isolate pertinent components of it, so that a judgment can be made about specific identifiable elements. Such a judgment may be expected to be quantitatively more objective — encompass a greater number of observable components in proportion to subjective components — than judgments about clusters of interactions. Evaluations generalized from such judgments may be expected to be more objective than evaluations generalized from a few judgments about categorized groups of interactions.

When judgments are made about groups of interactions classified according to one or several common elements, many individual observations, as well as many details of specific observations, are eliminated from consideration. The lessening of attention to individual observations leads to abstractness.

The abstractness, in turn, imposes limitations on objectivity in judgment, and leads to greater subjectivity than that elicited in judgment of clear, concrete, individual observations. That is, as the rater judges any one interaction:

1. She will consider the identity of the component of care about which she is making a judgment;
2. She will consider the patient's nursing care needs, both immediate and long-range;
3. She will consider care elements of the total episode of the nurse's interventive action in relation to the patient's needs;
4. She will consider the interacting elements which govern the nature of the content and approach utilized by the nurse.

When considering all of these factors in relation to a single, immediately observed interaction, the rater can consider not only their individual meaning and quality, but also the effects of the interactions among them and the influence on the quality of the care received by the patient. She can make decisions about quality with attention focused on the observed facts, related elements in the immediate situation, and a background of scientific information, with considerations uncluttered by personal impressions carried from earlier observations.

Factors and their interactions in a single observed intervention can be perceived on a level of concreteness that is impossible when factors and their interactions are identified in a generalization derived from recall of many individual interventions. Concreteness contributes to objectivity of judgment.

The nurse's intervention must be judged for its appropriateness in content and tone, not only in relation to needs identified beforehand, during assessment and development of the nursing care plan, but also in relation to the immediate situation and the mood of the patient.

Obviously, no completely objective, easily applied yardstick can ever be developed for measuring any one dimension or any set of dimensions of a single nurse-patient interaction.

It is impossible for a single instrument to encompass all the elements that are essential in measuring even one dimension of an interaction.

Nonetheless, proportionately more of the pertinent elements of an item of care can be included when one observed interaction is measured than it would be possible to include if measurement were made of a categorical item of care encompassing a large number of observations of many varied interactions.

Quite obviously, subjective thinking can be expected to focus more on pertinent facts when judgments are made about single concrete observations, with a relatively limited number of elements acting and interacting, than when judgments are made about a general category of nursing care actions with an infinite number of elements and interactions.

In the entire matter of measurement and evaluation of quality of nursing care, nurses must disabuse themselves of the idea that subjectivity is bad and objectivity is good. Both are unavoidable components of the process of measurement and evaluation, which, when recognized for what they are, make the values of good and bad inapplicable. To move forward purposefully in using evaluation for the many and varied purposes it can serve, nurses must recognize what they are attempting to do and the reason for doing it, and must have the confidence to know and the courage to show that they are capable of making informed judgments based on immediately observed facts and previously acquired knowledge. The Slater Scale is designed to facilitate focusing on relevant actions to be measured and effecting valid judgments, which are then reflected in the ratings in the Scale.

STANDARD OF MEASUREMENT

The standard of measurement of the Slater Scale is the quality of performance expected of a first-level staff nurse.

It should be noted that the term "performance" has been substituted for the term "care" used to identify the standard of measurement in earlier work on the Scale and employed in the Quality Patient Care Scale, which uses the same standard of measurement. The reason for the change is to allow more precise identification of the relationship of the performance of an action to the competence displayed in the performance. The general conception of the standard of measurement, "care expected of a first-level staff nurse," is not changed by this alteration in wording. The care provided by a nurse is to be measured in terms of the quality of the performance of the actions that constitute the care. The substitution is made in the belief that the term "performance," more than the term "care," assists the rater to focus definitively on the quality of the performance of actions composing the individual nurse-patient interaction.

THE MEANING OF "QUALITY OF PERFORMANCE EXPECTED OF A FIRST-LEVEL STAFF NURSE"

A major complication in the use of the Slater Scale is that none of the terms in the standard of measurement is defined. The reason is that the concept is too complex to be defined.

The justification for use of the concept, despite its indefinability, is that persons knowledgeable in the field hold common ideas of its meaning. For example, should two or more nurses, in conversation, use the phrase, "quality of performance expected of a first-level staff nurse," to discuss nursing care provided individual patients, each would readily envision nursing care planning, activities, and evaluations provided by a nurse for a particular patient or for individuals in a particular group of patients. Depending on the purpose of the consideration, few or many specific examples of care activities would be delineated, and there would be general agreement about the elements described as components of the nursing care expected of a first-level staff nurse.

The phrase "performance expected of a first-level staff nurse" identifies a very broad, general and encompassing concept; yet, in comparison with some very abstract concepts, such as liberty, freedom, or moral value, it is seen to be relatively concrete.

NO DEFINITION

The standard of measurement will not be defined:
- because persons knowledgeable in the field identify similar observable examples of "quality of performance expected of a first-level staff nurse";
- because there is general agreement about levels of quality of performance in nursing actions that make up care expected of a first-level staff nurse;
- because there is high inter-rater agreement for measurements made with both the Slater Scale and the Quality Patient Care Scale, both of which use the same standard of measurement;

● because delineation of the many elements and patterns of elements comprising the concept would be so involved and lengthy as to be unusable as a guide for making the measurements.

IDENTIFICATION OF THE STANDARD OF MEASUREMENT

Each nurse who rates the quality of care provided by individual nursing personnel in observed nurse-patient interactions or interventions will use her own conception of "quality of performance expected of a first-level staff nurse."

Each will envision a separate standard of measurement and magnitude of the yardstick she will use to measure the quality of the performance displayed in the observed nurse-patient interactions or interventions.

IDENTIFICATION OF FIRST-LEVEL STAFF NURSE

A first-level staff nurse is a nurse who, traditionally, is charged with responsibility for providing nursing care that is safe, adequate, therapeutic, and supportive in meeting the needs of patients.

A first-level staff nurse is one who, purportedly, is prepared for these responsibilities by one of the programs of nursing education that prepare individuals for state licensure as registered nurses.

Additional Comments

When they attempt to envision "quality of performance expected of a first-level staff nurse," raters protest that expectations differ for first-level staff nurses with varying educational backgrounds and experience. That is, expectations of performance by a nurse with a baccalaureate degree are different from expectations of performance by a nurse with an associate degree or a diploma in nursing. Expectations for nurses with two years' experience are different from those for a recent graduate.

To envision the standard of measurement, "quality of performance expected of a first-level staff nurse," the rater may be helped by thinking about what it is she will be measuring with the standard.

The standard of measurement, or "yardstick," will be used to measure the care elements of a variety of nurst-patient interactions or interventions.

For each measurement or rating, focus will be on the nature and quality of performance of the care in each interaction, and its appropriateness to the patient's care needs.

The focus will not be on the qualities of the nurse who is interacting nor on what is expected of that particular nurse.

The primary elements in the rating process are: (1) the *care* factor of the observed nurse-patient interaction and (2) the performance of *care* expected of a nurse (any nurse) charged with responsibilities for first-level staff nursing — adequate, safe, therapeutic, and supportive care.

The rater measures the quality of a single nurse-patient interaction by figuratively holding up the observed *care* of the interaction against the care performance of the standard of measurement as she has envisioned it. She will find that the observed care performance falls at some point on the yardstick, which is divided into 5 points, from care performance of a Best to care performance of a Poorest Nurse.

RATERS' AGREEMENT ON THE MEANING OF THE STANDARD OF MEASUREMENT

Findings from various testings of the Scale have demonstrated high inter-rater agreement in measurements of the quality of nursing care performance.

Agreement has been demonstrated in varied situations: in situations where care was being provided by staff nurses with similar backgrounds; in situations where most direct care of patients was provided by licensed practical nurses and nurse aides.

Agreement has been demonstrated in similarly varied situations for the Quality Patient Care Scale, which uses the same standard of measurement.

Extensive testings of the two scales demonstrate that nurses competent to judge the quality of nursing care performance displayed in nurse-patient interactions hold common conceptions of "quality of performance expected of a first-level staff nurse."

STANDARD OF MEASUREMENT HELD CONSTANT

As mentioned, the expectation of different levels of care from nurses with different educational backgrounds and experience causes some difficulties in envisioning "quality of performance expected of a first-level staff nurse" as a usable standard of measurement. In addition, these varying expectations lead raters to want to apply a flexible standard, one that will allow for different expectations for different subjects being measured. The aim seems to be "fairness" to all: to give all persons an opportunity to earn a high score or favorable measurement, not in terms of an established standard of performance but in terms of what could "reasonably" be expected of each. For example, it has been argued that it is unfair to measure the performance of a newly graduated nurse by the same standard that is used to measure the performance of a graduate nurse who has had three years of experience, or to measure a graduate from an associate degree program by the same standard used for one from a baccalaureate program; or to measure a sophomore by the same standard used for a senior. Different performances are expected from these various individuals; therefore, the reasoning goes, they should be measured by different standards. There is no need to describe in full detail the processes and standards of measurement proposed; nurses are familiar with many examples from personal experiences. Suffice it to note that such devices preclude comparing the performance of one individual with another or performances at different points in time.

A simple analog can help to make the point. If one were interested in knowing the heights of a seven-year-old boy and his father, the standard of measure- would be held constant, though their heights would be expected to differ — the same yardstick would be used to determine the measure of both heights. It is true that the boy, like some nurses, might prefer a flexible scale. Through use of the same standard of measurement, though expectation be that outcomes will vary, it is possible to demonstrate the difference at a particular point in time, and it is further possible to demonstrate growth of the boy over time. If a sliding scale were used, there would be no way of knowing what standard of measurement was being used at a particular time; there would be no way of knowing, without detailed instructions and calculations, whether measurements could or could not be compared.

It is only as the standard of measurement is held constant that measurements of various individuals can be compared to demonstrate differences or similarities in performance. For the Slater Scale, the standard of measurement is held constant and may be used to measure performance of any individual who intervenes, directly or indirectly, to provide nursing care for patients. It will yield reliable measurements that may be compared to show differences, similarities, and growth.

The standard of measurement is not changed to accommodate expectations of different outcomes; rather, the standard is held constant so that expectations of sameness or differences can be confirmed or demonstrated to be erroneous.

If attributes or features of different subjects are indeed different, comparison of each to a constant standard of measurement will reveal the difference. Comparison to flexible or different standards of measurement would fail to reveal reliable measurements of difference.

SECTION V

Tests of the Scale

Joel W. Ager and Mabel A. Wandelt

RELIABILITY

Inter-Rater Reliability

The ratees were 74 senior nursing students who had completed their 12 weeks of clinical experience. The 74 ratings were obtained from three different settings. Each student nurse was rated retrospectively on the Slater Scale by a pair of raters who had supervised and were familiar with their field performance. For one group of 20 students, one member of each pair of raters was a Wayne State University College of Nursing faculty member; the other was either a WSU graduate student or a clinical nurse specialist of the faculty serving as a resident staff member of the health care agency. For a second group of 20 students, the raters were pairs of regular instructors in a single clinical setting. For the third group, with 34 students, one of each pair of raters was the student's regular instructor and the other rater was a member from another clinical specialty faculty, who shared the clinical supervision of the ratee for the two weeks prior to completing the rating. The number of students rated by a given pair of raters ranged from 1 to 7. The interclass correlations for the three groups were .78, .75, and .72. The interclass correlation for the 74 student nurse ratings was .77. Interclass correlation, rather than the more usual correlation coefficient, was used for two reasons: (1) not all judges rated all nurses, as required by r; (2) because the Slater Scale attempts to measure absolute and not just relative performance, there should be agreement on level of performance as well as rank order. It should be noted that the interclass correlation will be lower than r, since variance due to disagreement on level is counted as error variance.

Internal Consistency

To the extent that the subscales of the Slater are tapping dimensions of performance that are to some degree distinct, we would expect within-scale inter-item correlations to be higher than inter-item correlation between scales. For the same reason, items should correlate higher, on the average, with their own total scale score than with the scores for the other scales.

Intercorrelations among items, scales, and total scores were computed for a sample of 250 diploma nursing students who had completed eight weeks of clinical experience in psychiatric nursing. Slater Scales were filled out retrospectively by the clinical instructors. The odd-even split-half reliability was .98. A factor analysis was performed on 71 of the 84 items having adequate sample sizes; the first principal axis factor accounted for 55 percent of total variance, yielding an estimate of Cronbach's coefficient α of $\sqrt{.55} = .74$. This may be an underestimate because of the unequal sample sizes for the various intercorrelations.

Stability

Data relevant to stability reliability of the Slater Scale were collected on 103 staff nurses at the Little Rock, Arkansas, Veterans Administration Hospital in connection with evaluation of a reorganization of the nursing service. Nurses were rated on the Slater initially and then six months later. Because of turnover among supervisory personnel who served as raters, the two ratings for each nurse were not necessarily done by the same person. The r on total Slater for the six-month interval was .60. Further results from this study pertaining to the program evaluation are discussed below.

VALIDITY

Construct Validity

Results from a factor analysis of inter-item correlations on 71 of the Slater items, based on 250 psychiatric nursing students (see Internal Consistency, above), resulted in a large general factor accounting for 55 percent of total variance. Using the criterion of retaining for rotation all factors having eigenvalues over 1, 12 factors were found. These accounted for 83 percent of total variance. On the varimax rotation, items from the six subscales showed some tendency to load on separate factors, except for subscales 5 and 6, and 2 and 4. Further rotational analysis of these data is perhaps warranted.

An additional bit of evidence concerning construct validity of the Slater comes from the Veterans Administration Hospital study cited above in the section on stability. Ratings on the 103 nurses after a six-month trial of the reorganized nursing service improved significantly (t = 4.2). The initial Slater mean was 2.86, with a standard deviation of .66, and the post mean, 3.09, with a standard deviation of .61.

Content Validity

The items on the Scale have been examined extensively and repeatedly by nurse educators and nurse practitioners with expertise in all major clinical areas. One such examination was done by clinical instructors (at least two from each specialty), who devoted six to ten or more hours each week for ten weeks. Each worked independently, and they met weekly to share ideas. As a result of their study, Item 41 was added to the original 83 items developed by Slater. There were some modifications of wording to enhance consistency of expression among the items, and some additional cues were suggested. This group of instructors indicated belief that the items on the scale are valid criterion measures of competencies needed by a nurse responsible for nursing care of patients. They proposed that the scope of the items is complete and that the items representative of the broad range of actions required in provision of nursing care. These instructors and many other users with both education and service concerns have reported that they find no nursing actions on behalf of patients or interactions with patients that cannot be rated on one or more of the scale items.

A second test of content validity was effected, coincidentally, when a faculty committee was planning for evaluation of the following curriculum objective: "Provide care to individuals, families, and groups, in a variety of settings, with utilization of the nursing process, incorporating scientific knowledge and humanistic concepts." In developing the three-phase definition of the terms as part of the process for identifying criterion measures relevant to the objective, many definitions of nursing were used. Extensive materials were drawn from the following sources: the State of Michigan Nurse Practice Act; the New York State Nurse Practice Act of 1972, and its accompanying definitions; definitions of "nursing process" from various sources in nursing literature, from 1965 to 1972; and the 1970 resolution of the American Association of Deans of College and University Schools of Nursing, in which the functions of professional nurses are identified. When criterion measures were drawn from the detailed pertinent general definition of the goal-identifying terms in this curriculum objective, it was possible to match 81 items from the Scale with them. Here another indication of the content validity of the Scale; the items provide for measurement of competencies required for performing actions that compose nursing care of patients.

Predictive Validity

Following are correlations of Slater Scale scores with various other measurements of nursing knowledge and performance:

- Instructor practice grades $r = .72$
- Instructor theory grades $r = .63$
- NLN Achievement scores $r = .54$
- Social Interaction Inventory $r = .69$

Discrimination

Raters discriminate between students on individual items, and among items for individual students. They discriminate between successive ratings on individual items for individual students. This latter was demonstrated convincingly during early testing of the Scale, when seven instructors did repeated measurements on sets of 55 to 60 students. Ratings were done for each student every two weeks for ten weeks.

These same sets of ratings provided evidence to demonstrate a second type of discrimination. Beginning with the fourth week, students were rated every two weeks during a twelve-week psychiatric nursing course; the three groups had their clinical experiences in three successive twelve-week periods in the same clinical setting. Scores were examined from the three groups of students, numbering 57, 58, and 57. For each group and for the combined group of 172 students, the mean scores increased and were significantly different for each successive two-week period.

The examination of these scores established that the Scale is sufficiently sensitive that a .4 difference in scores is significant and that student competencies acquired in as little as two weeks' time can be measured discriminatingly by the Slater Scale.

The pre- and posttest scores of the staff nurses in the Veterans Administration Hospital, mentioned above, further confirm the discriminatory capability of the Scale. The mean scores of 2.86 and 3.09 — a .23 difference — were significantly different.

SECTION VI

Measurement
for Evaluation

CONCEPTIONS ABOUT EVALUATION

There are certain concepts and processes fundamental to all evaluation endeavors. Awareness about some of them and suggestions for sequencing of the processes are offered to assist in planning a program of evaluation that is systematic and that holds assurance of accomplishing the purpose for which the project is instituted. Evaluation, rather than being considered as an entity that can be readily identified with a simple definition, must be viewed as a quasi-concept for which there are many valid conceptualizations. To serve the purposes of this discussion, several pertinent conceptualizations are delineated.

Measurement and Evaluation

With the view to eliminating the oft-used and faulty interchange of the two words "measurement" and "evaluation," it is well to begin by clearly identifying what measurement is, what evaluation is, and what their relationship to each other is. Both measurement and evaluation have two distinct meanings, related to the process of accomplishment of each.

Measurement, as a process, is the ascertainment of the dimensions, quantity, or capacity of something, usually by comparing a single phenomenon with a standard of measurement.

Measurement, as a result of this process, is the recorded number or symbol that represents the magnitude of the phenomenon in terms of the magnitude of the standard of measurement.

Evaluation, as a process, is the ascertaining or fixing of the value or worth (of a person or thing). The process includes application of considered judgment.

Evaluation, as a result of this process, is a generalization describing a judgment of the value or worth of a person or thing.

An *evaluation* is a generalization describing a judgment based on many *measurements*. Evaluation is subjective, as are all judgments and all generalizations. Measurement is objective; it is the noting of a single observable phenomenon. Clusters of related single, observed phenomena are the bases for generalizations, judgments, evaluations.

Use of Multiple Measurements

Evaluation is the determination, through use of multiple measurements, of the amount or worth of an entity, program, or process. Measurements used to determine an evaluation may be:

● individual observations of manifestations of a single criterion of a single variable;

- individual observations of several criterion measures for a single variable;
- individual observations of several criterion measures of several variables;
- individual observations of a single criterion measure of several variables.

For example: the evaluation of the success of a weight-watchers' program might be determined by multiple measurements of the single criterion measure, pounds, for the variable, weight. Or there might be multiple measurements of the criterion measures of pounds for the variable, weight, and inches for the variable, girth.

A diamond may be evaluated on the criterion measures germane to the variables size, hardness, color, purity of color, style of cut, and others.

The quality of nursing care may be evaluated on such criterion measures as efficiency, completeness, and timeliness, for the variables meeting the patient's physical needs, adaptation of care to needs of the individual patient, care calculated to prevent illness, involvement of the patient in his own care, and many others.

Securing Information

Evaluation is a process for securing information. The information can serve various purposes:

- for accountability pertinent to responsibility and commitment;
- for reporting accomplishment or achievement of a program or project;
- as a basis for planning improvements;
- for determination of change in a situation or in individuals, over time or following changes in setting or program;
- for determination of effects of changes introduced into a setting or of teaching programs.

Component of the Total Service or Production Program

Evaluation is a component of the total service or production program of any organization; yet, frequently, it is considered an individual entity and referred to as the evaluation program of the larger enterprise. This separating out may be a reason for some negative attitudes toward evaluation, for lack of understanding of its process and purpose, and for some faulty execution of various portions of the process. For example, one frequently occurring limitation in the evaluation endeavor, which may well stem directly from the separation of evaluation from the rest of the activities of a total enterprise, is the failure to involve all persons who make up the organization in all facets of the evaluation endeavor. It might be expected that, if evaluation were considered as much an on-going and integrated component of the enterprise as the service rendered or the goods produced, all personnel would necessarily have some part in the total evaluation process. And it is only as persons whose work and productivity are to be evaluated are informed about and involved in the total evaluation process that full benefits of the evaluation will accrue to the individuals and to the organization.

PROGRAM EVALUATION

Precision is a key to satisfactory evaluation endeavors. Relatively speaking, however, precision of measurements themselves are not so crucial to the success of an evaluation project as is precision in the delineation of purpose, identification of what is to be measured, and determination of relevant criterion measures. Not that preciseness of measurements may be ignored, but the most minutely precise measurements will serve not at all without precision in the delineation of the three components essential to any evaluation endeavor: statement of purpose, elements to be measured, and relevance of criterion measures.

Two Forms of Evaluation of a Program

The evaluation component of a program may take one of two major forms:

1. It may evolve from planning for, collecting, and interpreting measurements for purposes of comparisons – of different situations, of similar situations in different settings, of the "same" situation at different times, or of the "same" situation where planned change has been introduced.
2. It may evolve from planning for, collecting, and interpreting measurements for the purpose of determining the extent to which service program objectives are attained.

For the first and perhaps most frequently used form, the project planning is somewhat simpler than for the second. It is necessary merely to secure a measurement instrument that will produce the kinds of information wanted; to schedule times, places, and persons for making the measurements; and to analyze the findings by comparing the sets of measurements secured from the two or more situations, groups, or settings that are to be compared.

For the second form, determining the extent of attainment of program objectives, the process is considerably more complex. The planning must include consideration of the three purposes served by stated program objectives:

1. Objectives identify goals to be achieved.
2. Objectives serve as guides to the content of the program.
3. Objectives serve as guides to evaluation of the program.

IDENTIFICATION OF RELEVANT CRITERION MEASURES

The first step in utilizing the program objectives as guides to evaluation is to identify precisely the element or elements contained in the objectives that are to be measured: the words and phrases that identify the goal. This is perhaps the most neglected step in all evaluation project planning. Insufficient and imprecise planning is done. Precisely the measurements that may be expected to be relevant to each objective of the service program must be determined. First the following must be done:

- A number of criterion measures potentially germane to the objective must be identified.
- Decisions must be made about the ones to be used (frequently there will be a large, unwieldy number of relevant criterion measures).
- Tools that will secure measurements identified in the criterion measures must be found (or designed).

When these tasks have been completed, the process is similar to that appropriate for evaluations that seek information for making comparisons of groups or situations. The data will be analyzed to "compare" findings with goals delineated in each objective to determine the extent to which goals have been attained.

The most direct means to identifying the specific goals and the kinds of measurements that will indeed be relevant to the goals is through definitions of the goal-identifying terms in each objective.

Following is described a systematic process for assuring the relevance of the measurements to be used in evaluating the degree of attainment of objectives of any service program. The process encompasses definitive determination of the precise goals delineated in each objective and of criterion measures relevant to the goals sought. The process for determining the goals and criterion measures relevant to them is development of three-phase definitions of the goal-identifying terms in each objective.

The definitions of the terms serve two purposes:

1. assurance that an objective says what those responsible for the program intend it to say;
2. identification of criterion measures relevant to each stated objective.

Three-Phase Definition of Goal-Identifying Terms

The components of a three-phase definition are:

1. general or dictionary definition of each word in the term;

2. pertinent general definition, a definition specific to the intent of the planners — specific to the attribute, behavior, or situation declared in the objective to be an aim or goal of the program;
3. for-instance definition, a description of an observable phenomenon illustrative of the pertinent general definition and, in turn, of one or more of the general or dictionary definitions.

Essentially, a definition is an arbitrarily imposed description that allows common understanding.

Each of the three components of the definition of a term may be considered a definition that might stand alone. Yet, the combination of the three provides a useful description that enhances understanding because the descriptions move from a high level of abstraction and generality — the first-phase description will fit any "instance" — to a somewhat specific area between abstractness and concreteness — what, in general, the definer means by the term — to a level of concreteness — the pointing to a single observable phenomenon that provides a precise illustration of what the definer means by the term. A simple example of the three phases can serve as an aid to remembering the conception: A thing of beauty is a flower is a rose. The very general "thing of beauty" might refer to a sunset, a seascape, a sonata, a child. For this definer, the pertinent general description is a flower. The flower might be any one of scores of species of flower; for this definer, the for-instance description is a rose. The reader might use this simple illustration or develop one of his own that will come as readily to mind.

Varied Statements of an Objective

To provide a concrete frame of reference for describing the development of a three-phase definition and purposes to be served by the definition, three statements of objectives will be used. The statements seemingly have the same goal intent, yet each is delineated slightly differently from the others.

1. The program provides experiences that will promote development of skills in guiding the work of others.
2. The student will develop increased competence in guiding the work of others.
3. The student guides the activities of auxiliary personnel.

The three-phase definition will be developed for the goal-identifying term of the third objective. The first two statements will subsequently be used to illustrate other related points (pp. 75-77).

The objectives will be used to serve three primary purposes and to illustrate several other considerations germane to planning an evaluation of the attainment of program objectives. The primary purposes are illustrations of:

• development of a three-phase definition of terms;
• assurance that the objective says what the planners intend it to say;

● identification of criterion measures relevant to each stated objective.

ILLUSTRATING THE THREE-PHASE DEFINITION

The sample objective is: The student guides the activities of auxiliary personnel.

Phase 1: General or Dictionary Definitions of Words

● *Guide* – to show the way, to conduct; to lead; to direct. To direct the course of. To manage the affairs of, to govern. To influence the conduct or opinions of; to be a criterion for or motive of.
● *Activity* – energetic action or movement.
● *Auxiliary* – one who assists or helps; an assistant.
● *Personnel* – the body of persons employed by or active in an organization, business, or service.

Should a word or phrase of a term be one that connotes a complex concept, particularly an esoteric concept utilized in a certain discipline, the general definition should be sought in a dictionary or glossary of words developed for communication in and about the particular discipline or from writings in the discipline. For example: for anxiety, definitions would be sought in the literature of psychology; for nursing or nursing process, search would be in the literature of nursing; for wound infection, the literature of medicine or epidemiology; for community, the literature of sociology. For these words, as well as using a dictionary definition, the definer would go to specific literature from the discipline and select an encompassing definition that is consistent with his intent in using the word.

Phase 2: Pertinent General Definition

● A definition specific to the intent of the planner – specific to the attribute, behavior, or situation declared in the objective to be the aim or goal of the program.

The general or dictionary definitions of words in the statement of the objective may be obtained in any order or sequence without affecting the results or the amount of effort involved in doing the definition. Such is not the case when doing the pertinent general definition. The key to parsimony of effort and detail and to logical development of the pertinent general definition is to develop the definition of the goal-identifying term by beginning with the definition of the last word in the term and delineating the definition by incorporating descriptions of each word in the reverse order of its appearance in the term. This "rule" implies that a term to be defined for purposes of identifying criterion measures may be a single word or, as in most instances, may be composed of several words. The second phase of the definition will include descriptions of each word, but the portion of the pertinent general definition that will identify criterion measures will be the final portion when descriptions of all words composing the term have been incorporated into the description of what, in general, the definer means by the term. To illustrate, the goal-identifying term, "guides the activities of auxiliary personnel," is defined, beginning with the description of what the definer means by *personnel*.

Personnel — persons employed by a health care agency to provide nursing care services to patients for whose care the agency has assumed responsibility.

Auxiliary personnel — persons with various types of educational preparation for work in a particular field of employment; usually connotes the requirement of working under the supervision of professionals. Persons with various types of educational preparation for working in the field of nursing, but with less education than required for state licensure as a registered nurse, who are employed by a health service agency to provide care for patients under the supervision of registered nurses. Persons who contribute to the nursing care of patients through assisting registered nurses by actions performed both independently and in cooperation with others, all under direct or indirect supervision of a registered nurse.

Activities of auxiliary personnel — actions performed by persons with various levels of educational preparation for the purpose of meeting health care and treatment needs of patients for whose care the employing agency has assigned responsibility to a registered nurse. Actions are performed with and on behalf of the patient; they may be performed by the auxiliary person alone, with another auxiliary person, or with a registered nurse; they may range in complexity from very simple measures of daily hygiene to complicated therapeutic procedures; all actions will be done under direct or indirect supervision of the registered nurse.

Guides activities of auxiliary personnel — directs the actions performed by persons of various levels of educational preparation for the purpose of meeting health care and treatment needs of patients for whose care she — the registered nurse or registered nurse student — is responsible. Works with the auxiliary personnel to show the way to perform nursing care procedures. Leads work of one or more auxiliary persons by suggesting processes of care; by reminding them of needed care; by consulting them about planning care; by questioning them so as to enhance their competence and alertness in observing the patient's response to care and treatment, in assessing the patient's needs for care, and in many other ways.

Phase 3: For-Instance Definition

- A description of an observable phenomenon that is illustrative of the pertinent general definition and, in turn, of one or more of the general definitions.

Nurse K asks Nurse Aide J to describe his plan for handling drainage tubing and IV tubing when getting Mr. P up for his first time out of bed since his surgery.

Nurse R reviews with Orderly G his handling of Patient N when getting him ready for his breakfast; she suggests ways the tray might have been positioned so that Mr. N might have been more comfortable while eating and been less tired afterward.

LESSONS IN THE ILLUSTRATION

The sequence of listing the "lessons" is not intended to indicate order of significance either for stating the objectives or for defining the terms.

LESSONS GERMANE TO ASSURING
THE INTENT OF THE PLANNERS

Lesson 1. Identification of Criterion Measures

When the three-phase definition is complete, the next step in the planning for evaluation is the identification of criterion measures delineated in the pertinent general phase of the definition.

A *criterion measure* is an attribute, characteristic, or quality of a variable that may be measured to provide scores by which subjects or things of the same class may be compared with respect to the variable.

In the objective, "The student guides the activities of auxiliary personnel," the relevant variable is the "guiding" actions or behavior of the student. Among the attributes of guiding that are described in the pertinent general definition are: directs, demonstrates, shares work, questions, leads, reminds. As these attributes are being elicited from the pertinent general definition, others may come to mind; they should be listed along with those explicit in the definition (see Lesson 2, below).

The next step is to plan for securing measurements of the identified attributes. The for-instance phase of the definition provides examples of behaviors or actions displayed by the student that are evidence of achievement of the goal. Consideration of these suggestions leads to recognition that the measurements to be taken — the phenomena to be observed — will be in terms of whether the student does or does not display (performs or fails to perform) "guiding" actions and behaviors. The "score" for each measurement will be a number, hashmark, or check on a checklist; the ultimate form will be a number representing the frequency with which a student displayed guiding actions or behaviors.

Lesson 2. Stated Objective and Planner's Intent

When planning focuses on the exact nature of the measurements that may be expected to be derived for a single thing or subject that will be measured, it becomes clear just what information will be obtained from the planned measurement process. In this instance, the measurements will be frequencies of the student's performance of or failure to perform guiding actions. It may be surmised that planners of an educational program would be expecting learning of greater scope and would seek more definitive measurements of student learning in the area of guiding the work of auxiliary personnel than merely evidence of frequency of performance or failure to perform guiding actions, or even of frequencies of performance of particular types of guiding actions. Yet, the total frequency of guiding actions along with frequencies of specific categories of actions are the extent of the information indicated by the pertinent general definition as relevant evidence of attainment of the stated objective.

It is at this point that the planners will recognize that the objective, as stated, does not entirely express their intent. The planners, in this instance, may decide to modify their objective from the original statement to one including the word "effectively," as a means of expressing their more encompassing intent. This, in turn, would necessitate adding one more component to both the general and the pertinent general definitions and would require a new for-instance definition.

Phase 1: General or Dictionary Definition

Effective — having the intended or expected effect; serving the purpose. Producing or adapted to produce the desired impression or response. Producing a desired result or outcome.

Phase 2: Pertinent General Definition

Effectively guides the activities of auxiliary personnel — directs the actions performed by auxiliary personnel in a manner that results in the meeting of the health care and treatment needs of patients. Demonstrates care actions in such a manner that auxiliary personnel learn to perform them with little or no additional guidance as they provide care for patients. Involves auxiliary personnel in a manner that moves them to initiate care activities that will contribute to the adequate and improved care of the patient. Leads in a manner that encourages each person to develop and perform at the highest level of competence.

Phase 3: For-Instance Definition

Student reviews with the nurse aide the procedure for the first postoperative ambulation of Patient Jones, eliciting a description of the actions to be taken by the nurse, the nurse aide, and the patient; the sequence of the actions; and the observations to be made during the procedure. After responding to several lead-questions, the aide volunteers several items of information and suggests a modification of the usual sequencing of some actions because of the patient's complaint of unusual soreness in his right arm and shoulder. The patient is gotten out of bed, ambulated, and put back to bed with no untoward incident; he comments, after he is back in bed, that the experience did not cause nearly the pain he had expected and that he will certainly be less reluctant to get up the next time.

It should be noted that descriptions in the pertinent general definition flow from ideas about the intention of the planners, without thought of identification of criterion measures. Thinking is focused on the goal or outcome sought and expected to result from the program to be planned. Concern is directed toward criterion measures after the three-phase definition is complete, at which time the planners return to the pertinent general definition and draw from it the relevant attributes (criterion measures) that have been described as the planners' meaning of the goal-identifying term in their stated objective.

The pertinent general definition of "*effectively* guides the activities of auxiliary personnel" reveals that, now, concern is with the effectiveness of the nurse's guidance of the activities of personnel, and not merely with the fact of her performing the guiding actions. The evidence sought to demonstrate the extent of achievement of the objective must relate to the effectiveness of the nurse's guidance, not merely to the fact of her having guided. The variable of concern continues to be the guiding actions or behaviors of the student, but the planners have indicated interest in a particular aspect or component of guiding actions. The aspect with which they are concerned is effectiveness — in contrast to other aspects, such as speed or authoritativeness, which could conceivably be of interest to other persons examining guiding behaviors.

Review of even the abbreviated pertinent general definition reveals two categories of criterion measures (attributes) of effectiveness:

1. Effects for those guided:
    a. Personnel learn to perform.
    b. Personnel perform without direct supervision.
    c. Personnel understand reasons for actions.
    d. Personnel initiate care activities, and so forth.
2. Effects for patients:
    a. Health care and treatment needs of patient are met.
    b. Patient receives adequate care.
    c. Patient care is improved.
    d. Patient participates in own care, and so forth.

These illustrations serve to emphasize once more the impact of precision of statement and the difference a single word can have in expressing intention and in planning for kinds of measurements that will provide evidence of the attainment of the objective.

Lesson 3: Scope and Limits of Intent

The culminating portion of the pertinent general definition of the complete term, "effectively guides the work of auxiliary personnel," illustrates clearly the relevance of the definition to the concerns of the planners. In developing the culminating definition, the planners must make explicit what they intend the program goal to be – precisely what they mean by "effective." As defined here, effectiveness encompasses two major components: desired behaviors for the persons guided and desired patient care results. There might have been other meanings of "effective," such as the completion of work on time, the most economical use of supplies and equipment, and so on. Indeed, these suggestions may appropriately be added to the definition as delineated, which leads to still other lessons in the illustration (see Lessons 9 and 10, pp. 73-75).

Lesson 4: Limitation of the Number of Criterion Measures

Should the additional descriptions of the meaning of "effective" be added to the pertinent general definition of the goal-identifying term, as suggested in Lesson 3 above, there would be two immediate effects: (1) an increase in the number and variety of criterion measures, and (2) a necessary enlargement of the scope of the program designed to achieve the objective (see discussion p. 78).

In terms of the first effect, it would be necessary to add to the for-instance definition to identify specific observations that would provide measurements of each of the criterion measures – attributes or characteristics of effective guiding, as described in the expanded pertinent general definition. A greater variety of observations would have to be made, which in turn would require a more complex tool for recording the observations.

A further effect would be to require decisions about the criterion measures to be used. When an objective is stated as broadly as is this one, it is possible to delineate scores of potentially relevant criterion measures, which can lead to a very unwieldly set of materials. Their number may be restricted in various ways: (1) The Planners may limit what their intent is for the goal to be achieved, with the limitations reflected in the pertinent general definition; and (2) The decision may be made to use only selected criterion measures from among the boundless possibilities. Where the intended goal is broadly encompassing, it is good to provide considerable detail in the pertinent general definition and to select the most relevant and useful measures to be included in the measurement portion of the evaluation project. The detail in the definition will give greater assurance of inclusion of the more relevant criterion measures, and the selection of criterion measures will serve to eliminate some only tangentially relevant measures, as well as possible padding with redundant or overlapping measurements; there is no need for overkill.

LESSONS GERMANE TO THE PROCESS OF DEVELOPING THE THREE-PHASE DEFINITION

Lesson 5: Omission of Some Elements of the Dictionary Definition

Some components of dictionary definitions for various words are not included in Phase 1, the dictionary or general definition. When a particular meaning is obviously not relevant to the concerns of the planners, it is deleted (see Lesson 10). Caution should be exercised, however, lest meanings of subtle applicability be overlooked.

Lesson 6: Incomplete Pertinent General Definition

Each of the successive sections of the pertinent general definition is abbreviated, but there is adequate detail to illustrate the process, the value, and the use of this phase of defining a term. If the work were actually to be used to plan for measurements of the degree of attainment of the objective (which is not the purpose of this discussion), many more elements would be suggested in each of the sections of the pertinent general definition. But even when planning is being done "for real," the pertinent general definition is seldom exhaustively developed. Where objectives are broadly stated, an exhaustive pertinent general definition would be more lengthy than necessary. The idea is to develop the pertinent general definition in sufficient detail to identify the intent of the planners and to provide explicit identification of many relevant criterion measures and a base for inferring many more.

Lesson 7: Incomplete For-Instance Definition

The one for-instance definition serves to illustrate the process. Should a three-phase definition be exhaustively developed, there might be dozens of examples for each criterion measure delineated in the pertinent general definition. Such detail would be redundant.

The pertinent general definition must be sufficiently detailed to identify a considerable range of relevant criterion measures. The number and detail of the for-instance need only be sufficient to yield explicit specific observations that are examples of one or more of the criterion measures and to ensure that persons knowledgeable about the goals of the program would agree to the relevance of the criterion measures and the validity of each for-instance as an example of the measure. Where there are more than three criterion measures, it is necessary to do for-instances for only two or three of them. This will be sufficient to allow other persons equally familiar with the area of concern to supply for-instances for other criterion measures, should they be needed in later planning. If a tool already exists that will serve in making and recording observations relevant to the goal, there is unlikely to be any need for greater elaboration of for-instances. Should it be necessary to develop an observation-making and -recording tool, more for-instances will be adduced, either as part of the definition process or with reference to the definition as a part of the tool construction.

Lesson 8: Words to Be Used or Not to Be Used in Definitions

Exact words, synonyms, and terms from the dictionary or general definition should be used in constructing the description that comprises the pertinent general definition of a word or term. As in any definition, meaning becomes more explicit if repetition of the word being defined is avoided in the description. For brevity's sake, in pertinent general definitions of lengthy terms, it is reasonable to use an actual word from the term being defined in the later sections of the definition and where the fuller description has been repeated in several preceding sections of the definition. For example, in the illustration given above, the words "auxiliary personnel" are used in the final two sections of the pertinent general definition, after the more descriptive identification has been repeated in earlier sections (pp. 67, 69, 70).

Lesson 9: Integration of Words in the Reverse Order of Their Appearance in the Term

When the definition of a term is developed in a sequence in which the planners' meaning of each of the words is described in the reverse order of its appearance in the term, the full pertinent general definition evolves in an orderly fashion. The description from the previous word becomes a part of the description of the next word. The description from the first two words defined becomes a part of the definition of the term identified by the third word, and so on.

The usefulness of this process will become even more evident if the reader will digress to engage in a brief exercise of more-or-less trial and error. He should attempt to develop the pertinent general definition for the term, "effectively guides the activities of auxiliary personnel," without following the sequence key; that is, starting with the first word in the sequence, "effectively." It will immediately become obvious that, once the general definition of "effectively" is stated, there is no way to identify the particular meaning without using concepts from "guide"; then allusion to "activities" becomes necessary; and soon elements from "auxiliary personnel" are needed. Then, when all of these elements are used in the definition of "effectively" — and they must be, in order to describe the planners' particular intent — and the definer moves to the next word, "guides", he again finds the need to draw from the words appearing later in the term. With very brief experience in this pursuit, the reader will note that the resulting descriptions are jumbled, with additions occurring in no orderly fashion. Following this short exercise, when the reader returns to development of the pertinent general definition by working in the reverse order of each word's occurrence in the term, he will notice that there is no need for elements from words of the term other than those whose meanings have already been described. The reader will find that utilization of the elements from other words flows to the natural and orderly evolution of the completed pertinent general definition and that the definition clearly indicates the intent of the planners. Furthermore, on subsequent analyses of the definition, the criterion-measures relevant to evaluation purposes will be readily identifiable.

Lesson 10: Repetition of Words and Phrases from First Sections in
         Later Sections of the Pertinent General Definitions

As each new word is added to the developing pertinent general definition, words, synonyms, or phrases from the general definition of the word (Phase 1) are repeated and incorporated into the evolving pertinent general definition. The words utilized in the developing pertinent general definition are those that serve best to describe and explain the intent of the planners. For example, one meaning of the word "guide" is "to manage the affairs of; to govern." These words and phrases would not be incorporated into the pertinent general definition being created here since they are not likely to be descriptive of the intent of the program planners, who have as an objective, "The student effectively guides the activities of auxiliary personnel."

Lesson 5 suggests omitting obviously irrelevant elements from Phase 1, general definitions of the words composing the term, but it cautions about omitting elements that may have subtle relevance. It is during the process of delineating descriptions in the pertinent general definition that the definer considers more closely each of the elements in the general definition. It is here that final decisions are made about the use and relevance of each element of the general definition in making explicit the intent of the planners about the meaning of the goal-identifying term in the stated objective.

IMPRECISION REVEALED BY THE THREE-PHASE DEFINITION

Other Statements of the Objective

Two other statements of objectives that apparently are intended to identify the same goal outcomes for an educational program are:

1. The program provides experiences that will promote development of skills in guiding the work of others.
2. The student will develop increased competence in guiding the work of others.

It is not necessary to give the three-phase definitions for the crucial (goal-identifying) terms in either of these objectives to illustrate the discoveries that the planners would make as they defined the terms and the consequent modifications that would be carried out in the statements.

Even as the definers develop Phase 1 definitions of the first statement, they would discover that the goal expressed by the phrase "the program provides experiences" and the evidence needed to confirm achievement of the goal would be observations about types of experiences. Persons knowledgeable about writing program objectives would know this even before moving to planning for evaluation of achievement; those who did not recognize the flaw out of hand would discover it as they worked out the three-phase definition.

Broad General Terms versus Specific Terms

The planners may ignore the commitment to experiences and the need for measurements of the experiences in terms of their "promoting development of skills," and focus only on planning to elicit evidence of "skills in guiding the work of others." Should this be the course taken, the planners might well move to delineation of the pertinent general definition before recognizing the lack of precision in stating their intent. The first element to be recognized as imprecise would be the word "others." Immediately, they would see that use of the term "auxiliary personnel" would not lengthen the statement, yet would make their intent more explicit. As soon as the description of the intended meaning of "work" is begun, it is obvious that the statement of the objective can be made

more definitive by replacing "work" with "activities." When "skills" is defined,
it will be discovered that evidence of each skill must pertain to guiding actions
and behaviors, that skills themselves cannot be observed. This consideration is
analogous to the imprecision in the second stated objective and will be elabor-
ated in relation to it (see below).

Unnecessary Clutter in the Statement of Objective

The second objective is stated in terms advocated by many educational program planners. They delineate the goal through reference to the student's development of or possession of an ability (competence, skill). As stated above, when
the goal-identifying term is defined, it becomes obvious that the declared goal,
"development of skill (ability, competence)," cannot be observed directly. When
planners who use this type of statement of objective identify criterion measures
relevant to the goal, they usually ignore the term "develop" and delineate criterion measures of the "skill or ability." The criterion measures, in turn, are
guiding actions or behaviors, which are indirect measures of the skill or ability.
Now, there is not anything wrong with taking this route, except that it adds to
the complexity of the evaluation process, and it may well be considered imprecision of the statement of intent of the planners.

It may be presumed that the planners intend that the student will learn to do
— that, as the end result of the educational program, the student *will* perform
particular behaviors, not merely that he will *possess the ability* to perform them.
Since the prime evidence of the ability is the actual performance, and since the
goal is that the student will perform, it seems rather superfluous to construct the
statement of an objective so that the identified goal is student ability to perform,
rather than actual student performance. The two statements implicitly express
the same intent of the planners, but when the explicit goal-identifying terms are
defined and the relevant criterion measures identified, it is obvious that the inclusion of "develops ability (skill, competence)" clutters the statement of the
objective and markedly complicates the planning for securing relevant measures
of evidence of attainment of the objective.

Commitment Beyond Intent

One further note about precision of statement will be made with reference to
the second objective. Again, without need to work out the definitions of the term,
consideration of the term "increase" reveals that the planners may not have intended to commit themselves to providing evidence of the student's attainment
of the declared goal, "develop *increased* competence." When the pertinent general
definition moves to including the elements from the definition of "increase," it
will become clear that the planners have committed themselves to providing evi-

dence of change in the student's competence. At this point, the obvious becomes apparent—since a measurement is a single observation of a phenomenon, increase (change) cannot be directly measured. Change must be calculated from two or more measurements.

Following this realization, the planners may decide to alter the statement of the objective, declaring that they do not really mean to commit themselves to providing evidence of change in the student. They expect the student to change, but they do not wish to commit themselves to adducing evidence of this change. They are willing to substantiate the effectiveness of the program by showing that the student has achieved a stated goal, without providing evidence that she actually changed or increased certain behaviors.

On the other hand, if the planners indeed intend to demonstrate change as an outcome of the program, then the objective should be so stated, and planning should include identification of types of observations (measurements) that will provide data for calculating the direction and, possibly, the degree of change. Planning must also provide for ways and means to secure the needed measurements at two or more points in time.

OBJECTIVES AS GUIDES TO THE CONTENT OF THE PROGRAM

Essentially, the three-phase definition of the goal-identifying term in an objective serves two purposes: (1) assuring that the objective, as stated, says what the planners intend it to say, and (2) identification of relevant criterion measures. These two purposes relate to two primary purposes served by delineation of program objectives — identification of goals and guide to evaluation. Less directly, but just as meaningfully, the defining of terms contributes the third purpose served by the delineated objectives — guidance to the content of the program. The consideration of this factor was introduced in Lesson 4 (p.71). For the purposes of this essay, which is to assist in planning for evaluation of programs and and to provide guidance to the use of the Slater Scale for securing measurements that serve as evidence of attainment of objectives, it is not necessary to provide detailed examination of this factor. Brief mention is provided to round out the discussion of purposes served by delineated program objectives and to identify one more function of the three-phase definition of goal-identifying terms.

In the usual course of events, planners develop objectives, which identify the goals for their program; then they move to planning the content of the program designed to achieve the goals; and last, they undertake planning for evaluation of the program. The discussion of the three-phase definition repeatedly gives evidence that the planning of the program content would be greatly affected if the order of the proceedings were altered so that planning for evaluation replaced planning for content in sequence and became second in the work of program development. One example of this influence is provided by the suggestion concerning elaboration of additional descriptions to be included in the pertinent general definition (p. 71). As the planners develop the descriptions of precisely what they mean by "effectively guides," they identify the scope and limits of what they intend to accomplish by the program. In so doing, they identify the scope and limits of what the content of the program must be to assist the student to achieve the intended goals. Should the definition stand as delineated in the three-phase definition (pp. 66-68), the program would not have to include content to assist the student in learning the economical use of supplies or the conservation of time of auxiliary personnel. Should additions be made as suggested in Lesson 3 (p. 71), the planners must adapt their planning about program content to provide for the necessary learning experiences for the student.

When described in a reasonable sequence, as above, these lessons seem rather self-evident. But when planning for content precedes planning for evaluation and development of definitions of the goal-identifying terms, planning for content is frequently carried out that is unrelated to the intended goal of the planners, content needed to allow students to achieve the declared goal is frequently omitted, and the quantity and emphasis of particular content is frequently disproportional to the intent of the planners, a disproportion that may be in the direction of either excess or dearth. Furthermore, the planners may find that there is no way to provide content that will permit achievement of the stated goal.

Perhaps most frustrating of all, planners may discover that there is no way they can secure measurements of a goal as it is stated in the objective. An example of the latter occurred when a faculty delineated as a curriculum objective: "Student contributes to the improvement of nursing standards and practice." The general definition of "standard" suggests – and the pertinent general definition of "improvement of nursing standards" confirms – that it is not possible to provide sufficient experiences for students to learn, directly, to make contributions to the improvement of standards. It is conceivable that students might indirectly learn this to a limited degree. But, as the pertinent general definition evolved, it became quite obvious that there would be no opportunity for securing measurements for the majority of students. Students may well contribute to improvement of nursing practice so that particular standards may be achieved, but students do not have opportunities to contribute to the improvement of nursing standards. The faculty had to find some other words to express what they intended as goals for the process of professionalization of students. Quite obviously, the objective as stated would not serve for planning a particular program (curriculum) content. The solution selected by the faculty was to drop the word "standards" from the stated objective and to plan that student learning for the improvement of nursing practice would emphasize the relationship between improvement of practice and attainment of established nursing practice standards. They would help students to understand the relationship between practice and standards, and the responsibilities of professional persons for promoting practice that will measure up to established standards. Such learning could be expected to provide students with a base for their later contributions as professionals to the improvement of standards. Such decisions provide bases for planning curriculum and course content that is realistic and consistent with stated goals.

To repeat, it is not necessary for the purpose of this essay to elaborate further the planning of program content. Suffice it to point out that reversing the usual order of program planning in relation to the second- and third-named purposes served by delineated program objectives would provide for more systematic procedure in planning, would preclude the need to redo portions of planning, and would provide greater assurance of inclusion of pertinent content in the instruction component of the program. Even if planners do not use the mechanism of development of a three-phase definition of the goal-identifying term, but determine relevant criterion measures through some other process, planning for evaluation of achievement of goals before planning for content contributes to more orderly evolution of the total program and eliminates the need to correct erroneous planning. The development of three-phase definitions makes the suggested sequencing for program planning an even more reasonable and systematic procedure.

The Essay as Background

The Slater Scale was designed to provide measurements of clinical nursing competence. It may be used to obtain measurements of quality of nursing performance in any setting in which nurse-patient interactions occur. The Scale provides for securing measurements of a large variety of nursing actions and behaviors. The measurements so derived can be used to evaluate the level of a nurse's competence overall and levels of competence displayed in particular areas of care, such as psychosocial and physical care. They can serve, also, to determine level of attainment of various individual program objectives. The first two evaluation scores are obtained through the organizational arrangement of the Scale. The evaluation of achievement of program objectives must be designed by the program planners.

Measuring Attainment of Objectives

The process for using measurements from the Slater Scale to determine the level of achievement of a set of objectives is introduced on pages 64-65 of the Essay.

1. Criterion measures relevant to each objective are delineated in the pertinent general definition of each goal-identifying term.
2. The most expressly and directly relevant criterion measures are pulled from the definition and placed in a listing for ready reference.
3. Items on the Slater Scale are reviewed and those that match the listed criterion measures for each objective are identified.
4. Listings are made of the numbers of the Scale items that correspond to criterion measures for each objective.

Explanation

The planners will find it helpful to use the Cue Sheet section of the Scale for these tasks. They will discover that the Scale items correspond to the criterion measures of the pertinent general definition and that the cues correspond to the for-instance units of their definitions. Incidentally, the reverse of the latter process may also serve; that is, cues can be a source of for-instances for the third phase of the definition of goal-identifying terms.

When evaluation time comes and completed Slater Scale ratings for students have been secured, a clerk may calculate the levels of achievement of each objective by pulling the scores from the items listed as corresponding to criterion measures for each individual objective. For example, for the illustrative objective in the Essay, "The student effectively guides the activities of auxiliary personnel," it will be found that nine items correspond to the criterion measures:

Items

61	69	81
63	76	82
65	78	83

The ratings from these nine items would be added and a mean score calculated. This will yield an evaluation level of achievement of the student with regard to that objective. The same process would be followed to determine level of achievement of each of the objectives of the program.

The scores for a group of students would then be used to calculate an overall level of achievement of the particular objective, which would provide an evaluation of the success of the program.

Uniformity of the Process Regardless of the Scope or Purpose of the Program

The term "planners" has been used to refer to program planners. The process for planning the evaluation component of a program is the same regardless of the scope of the program. Where planning is done for a program of the scope of a preservice educational program leading to a diploma or degree, the Slater Scale will not provide relevant measurements of some of the objectives of the program, but only those objectives whose goals involve aspects of clinical nursing practice. Where the "program" is of the scope of a clinical course, the Slater Scale may be expected to yield measurements relevant to all objectives for the course, with the Scale items providing from 3 or 4 to as many as 30 measurements relevant to a single objective.

The discussion in the Essay and this discussion have referred directly to the student and formal education programs. Yet, the processes and planning are the same whether the concern of the program is education or service. Relevant criterion measures are determined through the same process of defining the goal-identifying terms of each objective, and for-instance definitions are constructed to provide concrete examples of the intent of the program planners. Planning then moves to decisions about possible sources of evidence of the attainment of the goal, and then to search for a tool for securing and recording the observations that will constitute the evidence.

The reader is reminded that evaluation programs are most frequently executed with a view to comparing sets of scores to determine the effect of changes in the program, changes in individual behaviors resulting from educational programs, or similarities and differences in various settings or among persons with varied attributes. In both service and educational programs, some evaluations are done to determine the extent to which stated objectives of the program have been achieved. The Slater Scale will provide measurements to serve all of these purposes. The above describes a direct and systematic method for using measurements from the Scale as measurements of criteria relevant to the declared program objectives.

SLATER SCALE SCORES AND ACADEMIC COURSE GRADES

Some instructors, new to manipulating quantitative measurements, particularly quantitative measurements that are conversions from descriptive measurements, find it difficult to envision the use of measurements secured with the Slater Scale as a basis for reporting student attainment in terms of the academic grading system. Were the Scale measurements to be used with sophomore students, it is reasonable to expect that no student would receive a score above 3.2, and most would be much below this. Would this mean that no student would receive a grade above a C or average grade? Not so! The subunit on the scale of measurement, which descriptively is identified as "average" staff nurse, cannot be equated with the idea of a C that is descriptively classed as "average" on the academic grading scale of A to E.

Transformation of Scores to Grades

The appropriate procedure for transforming Scale scores to academic grades is as follows. The scores for all of the students in a class should be arranged in rank order from highest to lowest. In most instances, given ten or more students, the scores will tend to fall into clumps along the continuum. The following is an arrangement, in summary, of two sets of hypothetical scores:

Sophomores (Range: 3.1 to 1.4)	Academic Grade	Seniors (Range: 4.8 to 2.3)
3.1-2.7	A	4.8-4.4
2.5-2.1	B	4.2-3.9
2.0-1.5	C	3.6-3.0
<1.5	D	2.8-2.5
	E	<2.5

Note: The two arrays of figures are not an established pattern of equivalents; rather, they are illustrative. Each instructor will construct her own pattern of Slater Scale score equivalents for academic grades, based on the experience of the group of students being rated. Such a plan provides for ranking students in relation to the learning achieved by their peer group. It does not ascribe grades in relation to an arbitrary pattern of equivalents, based on preconceived expectations.

In this process, students with high scores are ascribed academic grades indicating high achievement; those with lower scores receive lesser grades. The sophomore with a score of 3.1, the highest achieved by her peers, receives the highest academic grade, an A. A senior who receives a score of 3.1, on the other hand, is given the academic grade of C.

This example demonstrates concretely the ability of the Slater Scale to provide measurements by which the student can see evidence on her own growth. The student who has maintained an average academic grade of A throughout her program knows only that she has continued to maintain an A level of performance. With the Slater Scale measurements, the same student can see her own growth through the changes in competencies scores, beginning at 3.1 and increasing to 4.4 or better, when she is a senior.

This description of the use of the scores and their logical conversion to serve academic purposes can assist instructors and other raters to adhere to the constant standard of measurement — performance expected of a first-level staff nurse — without regard to what might be expected of the ratee. There is one further exercise that can help raters to adhere to the standard of measurement, rather than feel compelled to rate in relation to what is expected of the individual being rated. The rater might read through the total list of items and place a check alongside each item for which the ratee could not possibly perform at a level of competence expected of a first-level staff nurse. For example, with regard to Item 2, "Is a Receptive Listener," a new nurse aide or a sophomore student may be expected to be able to perform at the same level as a Best Staff Nurse. In contrast, with regard to Item 13, "Utilizes Healthy Aspects of Patient's Personality," there is no way that a new nurse aide or a sophomore student could possibly perform at the level expected of a Best Staff Nurse. If the rater will check through all the items and review these designations prior to doing ratings for nurses and for whom she holds different expectation levels, she will find it easier to shift from the generally established pattern for rating nursing care actions (that is, rating on a sliding scale) to rating in relation to the standard of measurement held constant for all ratees.

Raters, as they adjust to using the constant standard of measurement of the Slater Scale, will find it helpful, too, to bear in mind that, when they rate an item on the Scale, they are not rating an individual, per se — they are holding a unit of patient care against the standard of measurement and obtaining a measurement of the magnitude of that one item of care; that they will be obtaining individual measurements of 60 or more items of care; and that these measurements will yield an evaluation level of the competence of the individual person. The individual measurements can be more or less depersonalized, with the measurement being an observation and judgment about an element of care and the ratee viewed as the vehicle of the particular element being measured at a given time. The evaluation of the ratee as an individual emerges from the calculations of the evaluation score from the many socres of quasi-isolated elements of care. The evaluation of the nurse ratee will truly be a "generalization describing a judgment based on many observations or measurements."

Others' Experiences
with the Slater Scale

HOSPITAL DIPLOMA SCHOOL

Faculties in five 16-week clinical courses decided to use the Slater Scale as part of end-of-course evaluation. The evaluation phase of their courses included postclinical evaluation conferences with each individual student. In previous experience, these conferences required one hour each, with one or two requiring from one and one-half to two hours, while the student argued about why she had received the rating she did. During the first week of the 16-week clinical courses, the students were supplied with copies of the Slater Scale, including the Cue Sheet and instructions for use, and were told that the Scale would be used in their evaluation. With the use of the Scale, it was found that not a single postclinical evaluation conference (25 instructors and 172 students) lasted more than one-half hour. Students' remarks were:

• Yes, I knew I was doing well in that area.
• I know I have to work more on that aspect of care.
• Why have we never been evaluated like this before?
• Now, I know what nursing is really about.

Instructors' comments included:

• It is so much easier to help students understand and plan.
• I have never before looked at my students as I do now.

LARGE GENERAL HOSPITAL NURSING SERVICE

There was a plan to institute a complete change in the nursing service administration. Six measurement devices were used to determine changes in nursing care; pre- and postmeasurements were done on 100 staff nurses. The Slater Scale yielded data that demonstrated significant differences in pre- and postscores.

Those who did the ratings complained no more about using the Slater Scale than about using any of the other instruments — they did not volunteer that they liked the Slater better, but they did not say that they liked it less!

MASTER'S THESIS

In a study titled, "Baccalaureate Graduates and Quality of Performance in Functional and Unit Management Assignments," Christman tested the following hypothesis: The quality of performance of baccalaureate graduate nurses working in functional patient care assignment settings is lower than that of those employed in unit management patient care assignment settings. The hypothesis was supported by scores secured with the Slater Scale.

In addition to providing quantitative measurements that can serve to test hypotheses, the Scale also provides descriptive data that are of interest to persons concerned with the quality of nursing care of patients and its improvement. Christman identified the areas of teaching, rehabilitation, and involvement of the patient in his own care as needing strengthening in both settings in which her study was conducted.

In her study, Christman makes the following comment:

> There is one additional factor that the writer as the observer feels should be expressed. During the data collection, it appeared to this observer that the Slater Nursing Competencies Rating Scale more easily evaluated the nurse's ability in practicing the *art* of nursing than it did the *science* of nursing. It also seemed that the subjects could achieve a high level of performance as rated by the Slater Scale regardless of their understanding, or nursing science knowledge. It was felt that part of this ability to interact with patients was a function of the individual subject's personality. It must be recognized, however, that part of this ability may be due to the individual subject's knowledge of human social behavior in health and illness and how well she was able to utilize such knowledge. It was difficult to determine with the Slater Scale what part of the interaction was based on knowledge and what part of the information was utilized to further the patient's care on an individual personality basis. It should be recognized that part of the inability to identify use of information may have been a function of the time element. The subject may have utilized the information at a later time after the observation period was completed. Repeated observations or a retrospective evaluation after a prolonged period of observation would more likely reveal whether the nurse did or did not utilize information gained from the patient during an interaction. The writer, however, still feels the need to question the sensitivity of the Slater Scale to the subject's knowledge of nursing science, particularly in the shadowing type of observation evaluation.

It is suggested that the final sentence of this comment is the key to the author's lack of ease with the sensitivity of the Scale for measuring the scientific knowledge component of the ratee's competence. No users who have done retrospective ratings have voiced questions about this aspect of the scale's applicability. Several users were asked about their experience in relation to it; each reported that she felt entirely confident in her own inclusion of the element of scientific knowledge as she made judgments and ascribed ratings to subjects for whom she had done retrospective ratings.

This does not mean that Christman's comment should be ignored or summarily dismissed. It may be of interest to cross-validate measurements obtained with the Slater Scale with measurements obtained with various tests of scientific knowledge, including teacher-made nursing tests, NLN Achievement tests, and tests used in courses in the germane basic sciences.

PRIMARY CARE NURSING

The Slater Scale, as well as the Quality Patient Care Scale, was used to secure measurements in a demonstration project titled "Evaluation of a Model Project to Increase the Quality of Nursing Care by Introducing the Concept of Primary Nursing." The two hypotheses were:

1. The mean scores derived from the Quality Patient Care Scale, the Slater Nursing Competencies Rating Scale, and the Phaneuf Nursing Audit will be higher for the experimental unit than for the control unit.
2. As the nurse level progresses from staff nurse to senior staff nurse to primary care nurse to clinical unit coordinator, the mean scores on the Slater Scale will be higher.

The first hypothesis was supported by data from all three tools mentioned; data from the Slater Scale supported the second. Felton lists the following advantages and disadvantages for the tools.

Advantages:

1. Allow reflection of better than expected performance, providing for rewarding reinforcement.
2. Allow identification of the actions that accounted for attainment of the goal of improving nursing care.
3. Allow analysis of interrelations among sets of data.
4. Categories of the Slater and Qualpacs relate to each other.
5. Address the underlying theoretical premises of the PCN rather than only its operation in place and time.

Disadvantages:

1. Need further analysis for construct validity.
2. Expensive in skill, time, and resources.

Among her recommendations, Felton proposes: "The Slater Scale should be instituted as a tool to evaluate nursing competencies and as a basis for assignment of nursing levels.

EFFECTIVENESS OF NURSING ASSESSMENT TOOLS

The Slater and Qualpac scales will be the major evaluation tools used in the study conducted by the State University of New York at Buffalo of the effectiveness of the Systematic Nursing Assessment of Patient-Family (SNAP) tools for improving nurse competencies and improving the quality of care provided patients. This study is designed as a three-year project in which the SNAP tools will be tested in hospital and community health agencies; the Slater and Qualpac scales will be used to secure pre- and postmeasurements. The project will be conducted under the guidance of Dr. Ruth T. McGrorey, principal investigator, and Miss Deane B. Taylor, project director.

A GENERALIZATION

The foregoing are but a few of the uses that others have made of the Slater Scale. There are many schools of nursing — baccalaureate, diploma, associate degree — that use the Scale. Some employ it in one or two clinical areas; others in all clinical areas.

There are nursing services in hospitals and nursing homes who use the Scale in annual evaluation of staff, and some utilize it as part of their in-service education programs to determine effectiveness and to identify areas of needed focus for future projects. Still others use it to secure information to serve various purposes in their quality assurance programs.

Several students have used the Scale as one of the measuring tools for data collection in their doctoral studies.

Wherever there is need for information, quantitative or descriptive, about the competencies displayed by nurses as they provide care for patients, the Slater Nursing Competencies Rating Scale can be expected to contribute in a large way to the securing of usable and useful information.

Glossary

DEFINITIONS OF WORDS GERMANE TO THE EVALUATION OF HEALTH CARE

Prepared by Mabel A. Wandelt as part of a paper, "Evaluation of Quality of Nursing Care," read at a Conference on Research on Nurse Staffing in Hospitals, Fredericksburg, Virginia, May 23-25, 1972.

DEFINITION An arbitrarily imposed description that allows common understanding.

EVALUATE To ascertain or fix the value or worth of. To examine and judge. To evaluate implies considered judgment in setting a value on a person or thing.

MEASURE To ascertain the dimensions, quantity, or capacity of. To mark off, usually with reference to some unit of measurement.

EVALUATION A generalization describing a judgment based on many measurements.

EVALUATION A process by which information is gathered as a basis for improvement.

QUALITY A characteristic or attribute of something; excellence; superiority, degree or grade of excellence.

STANDARD Something used by general agreement to determine whether a thing is as it should be. An agreed-upon level of excellence; An established norm.

MEASUREMENT A comparison of a single phenomenon with a standard of measurement; the recorded number or symbol that represents the magnitude of the phenomenon in terms of the magnitude of the standard of measurement.

STANDARD OF MEASUREMENT An object which, under specific conditions, serves to define, represent, or record the magnitude of a unit.

UNIT OF MEASUREMENT A precisely defined quantity in terms of which the magnitude of all other quantities of the same kind can be stated.

JUDGE To form an idea or opinion about (any matter). To think or suppose.

JUDGMENT The mental ability to perceive and distinguish relationships or alternatives; the critical faculty; discernment. The capacity to make reasonable decisions, especially in regard to practical affairs of life; good sense, wisdom.

SUBJECTIVE   Of, affected by, or produced by the mind or a particular state of mind. Of or resulting from the feelings or temperament of the subject or person thinking, rather than from the attributes of the object thought of, as a subjective judgment.

SUBJECTIVITY   The tendency to consider things primarily in the light of one's own personality. Concern with only one's thoughts and feelings.

OBJECTIVE   Of or having to do with a material object as distinguished from a mental concept, idea, or belief. Having actual existence or reality. Uninfluenced by emotion, surmise, or personal prejudice. Based on observable phenomena; presented factually.

MEASUREMENT   The objective process of ascertaining a dimension through observation of a phenomenon.

EVALUATION   The subjective process of ascertaining or fixing a value through considered judgment.

CRITERION   A quality, attribute, or characteristic of a variable that may
MEASURE   be measured to provide scores by which subjects of the same class can be compared in relation to the variable.

VARIABLE   A measurable or potentially measurable component of an object or event that may fluctuate in quantity or quality, or that may be different in quantity or quality from one individual object or event to another individual object or event to another individual object or event of the same general class.

References and Bibliography

REFERENCES AND BIBLIOGRAPHY

Brunner, Jerome. The skill of relevance or the relevance of skills. *Saturday Review*, April 18, 1970, pp. 66 ff.

Christman, Norma J. "Baccalaureate Graduates and Quality of Performance in Functional and Unit Management Assignments." Unpublished master's thesis, Wayne State University, 1969.

————. "Clinical Performance of Baccalaureate Graduates," *Nursing Outlook,* 19 (January 1971): 54-56.

Felton, Geraldene. "Evaluation of a Model Project to Increase the Quality of Nursing Care by Introducing the Concept of Primary Care." Early draft of a report, 1974. Quoted with permission, *Nursing Research* 24 Jan–Feb, 1975, pp. 27-32.

Gardner, Eric F., and Thompson, George G. *Syracuse Scales of Social Relations.* Yonkers-on-Hudson, N.Y.: World Book Company, 1959.

Jump, G. L., and Perkins, D. M. "Reliability and Item Analysis of an Evaluation Tool." Unpublished masters thesis, Wayne State University, 1965.

Wandelt, M. A., "Evaluation of Quality of Nursing Care," *Research on Nurse Staffing in Hospitals,* Report of the Conference, DHEW Publication No. (NIH) 73-434. Washington, D.C.: U.S. Government Printing Office, 1973. pp. 125-132. The glossary of terms germane to measurement and evaluation was developed as an accompaniment for this paper.

————. *Guide for the Beginning Researcher.* New York: Appleton-Century-Crofts, 1970. p. 322. The discussion of the three-phase definition of terms (pp. 85-109) is a revision and evolvement of an idea first described herein.

————. *Outcomes of Basic Education in Psychiatric Nursing.* Detroit: Wayne State University College of Nursing, 1966. p. 71. It was a part of the study reported here that the Slater Nursing Competencies Rating Scale was developed.

————, and Ager, J. W. *Quality Patient Care Scale.* New York: Appleton-Century-Crofts, 1974. p. 82.

DATE DUE

MAY 9			
APR 1 9 1979			
APR 2 8			
DEC - 9 1981			
DEC 1 '00			
FEB 7 '01			
2/26/01			
			PRINTED IN U.S.A.
GAYLORD